This revision guide is matched to the new single award OCR GCSE Additional Science B specification (J641), from the Gateway Science Suite.

The guide is designed to reflect the structure and ethos of the specification; it focuses on scientific explanations, theories and models, and explores the impact of science on society.

As a revision guide, this book focuses on the material on which you will be tested in the exams and covers the content of the six modules: Biology 3, Chemistry 3, Physics 3, Biology 4, Chemistry 4 and Physics 4.

You will have to sit two exams. An overview is provided in the table below, with details of where the relevant material can be found in this guide.

Although it does not directly cover the Skills Assessment (Research Study, Data Tasks and Practical Skills), which is marked by your science teacher(s), the information provided in this guide should help you to complete these activities.

The contents list and page headers clearly identify the separate modules, to help you revise for each paper individually, and the pages are colour-coded so that you can easily distinguish between Biology (green), Chemistry (orange) and Physics (blue).

This guide can be used to revise for both the Foundation and Higher Tier exam papers.

> **(HT)** Content that will only be tested on the Higher Tier papers appears in a coloured box, and can be easily identified by the symbol **(HT)**.

You will find a glossary at the back, providing clear definitions of key words and phrases, together with a copy of the periodic table for reference.

Don't just read the info — learn actively! Jot down anything you think will help you to remember, no matter how trivial it may seem, and constantly test yourself without looking at the text.

Good luck with your exams!

Authors: Jacquie Punter (Biology) is an expert in biochemistry, and has taught biology at Key Stages 4 and 5 for over 17 years. She has also taught health and social care and has an excellent understanding of the practical applications of science and its impact on society.

Steve Langfield (Chemistry) has been a science teacher for over 20 years and is an experienced examiner and moderator. He currently works as a science coordinator at a designated Specialist Science School, at the forefront of innovation in science and mathematics.

Robert Johnson (Physics) is a full-time teacher of physics at a respected co-educational public school. He has an innovative approach towards teaching, which makes physics – sometimes considered a dry and dull subject – relevant and interesting.

Project Editor: Rachael Hemsley
Editor: Rebecca Skinner
Cover and concept design: Sarah Duxbury
Designer: Richard Arundale

ISBN-10: 1-905129-73-4
ISBN-13: 978-1-905129-73-7

Published by Lonsdale, a division of Huveaux Plc.

Title	What is Being Assessed?	Duration	Weighting	Total Mark	Page Numbers
Unit 1	Modules B3, C3 and P3	1 hour	33.3%	60	4–53
Unit 2	Modules B4, C4 and P4	1 hour	33.3%	60	54–101

Contents

Contents

Molecules of Life

Cells

The fundamental processes of life take place inside cells. Below is a typical animal cell:

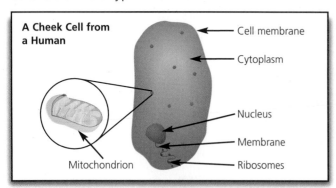

A Cheek Cell from a Human
- Cell membrane
- Cytoplasm
- Nucleus
- Membrane
- Ribosomes
- Mitochondrion

- Most chemical reactions take place in the **cytoplasm**. (It may contain mitochondria which is where most energy is released in respiration.)
- The **cell membrane** controls movement into and out of the cell.
- The **nucleus** contains the genetic information and controls what the cell does. It has a membrane extending from it, onto which ribosomes are attached.
- Protein synthesis (making proteins) takes place in **ribosomes**.
- Respiration takes place in the **mitochondria**, providing energy for life processes.

DNA

The nucleus of each cell contains a complete set of **genetic instructions**. The information is carried by **genes** on **chromosomes**, which are made from a chemical called **DNA** (deoxyribonucleic acid).

A DNA molecule is made of two strands coiled around each other in a **double helix** (spiral). The genetic instructions are in the form of a chemical code made up of four **bases**. These bases bond together in pairs, forming the cross-links (like rungs on a ladder) which hold the two strands of DNA together.

Before a cell divides (see p.12), it replicates (copies) its DNA to make sure that the new cells each contain a complete set of genetic information. This is how genetic instructions are passed on.

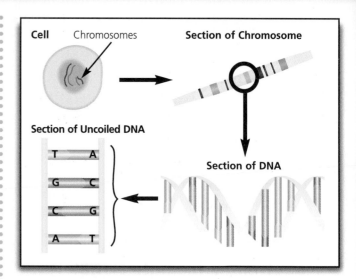

Cell — Chromosomes — Section of Chromosome

Section of Uncoiled DNA
- T — A
- G — C
- C — G
- A — T

Section of DNA

Protein Synthesis

DNA controls which proteins a cell synthesises (makes). Each gene codes for a particular protein.

Proteins are made up of chains of amino acids. The cell uses the amino acids that we get from food to construct them. Proteins are essential for the growth and repair of cells.

DNA Fingerprinting

Each person's DNA is unique, which means it can be used for identification. This technique is called **DNA fingerprinting**. For example, a crime suspect's DNA can be compared with a sample of blood found at a crime scene. A positive identification may lead to their arrest, whilst a negative identification might eliminate them from police enquiries.

Below is an illustration of how DNA can be compared.

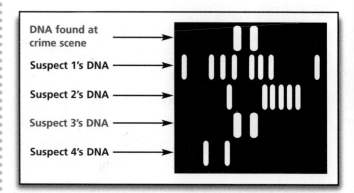

- DNA found at crime scene
- Suspect 1's DNA
- Suspect 2's DNA
- Suspect 3's DNA
- Suspect 4's DNA

The unique DNA fingerprint from the blood sample found at the crime scene matches exactly with the DNA fingerprint of Suspect 3.

More on DNA

The four bases in DNA are A (adenine), C (cytosine), G (guanine) and T (thymine). A always bonds with T, and C always bonds with G on opposite strands of the DNA molecule.

Uncoiled DNA Molecule – the bases code for the protein

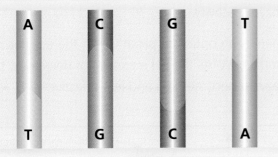

Double Helix Strands of DNA

More on Protein Synthesis

The sequence of bases in a gene represents the order in which the cell should assemble amino acids to make the protein. A group of three bases represents one amino acid in a protein chain. Each protein has a different function.

The liver can produce some amino acids by changing the structure of other amino acids. This process is called **transamination**. We can get the full range of amino acids by eating first class (animal) proteins. **Essential amino acids** are the ones we must get from our diet, because the body cannot make them.

More on Genetic Instructions

A cell can make an exact copy of its DNA molecule in the following way:

1. The double helix 'unzips.'
2. New bases pair up with the exposed bases on each strand.
3. An enzyme bonds the new bases together to form complementary strands.
4. Two identical pieces of DNA are formed.

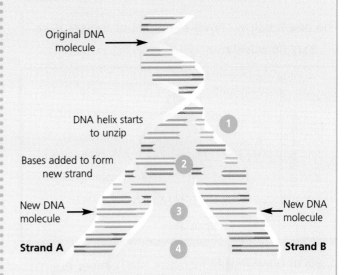

Original DNA molecule

DNA helix starts to unzip

Bases added to form new strand

New DNA molecule

New DNA molecule

Strand A

Strand B

The two new DNA molecules produced are genetically identical since their bases are complementary. Strand A has made a copy of strand B, and strand B has made a copy of strand A.

More on DNA Fingerprinting

To make a DNA fingerprint, a sample of DNA is needed. These are the steps taken:

1. **Isolation** – DNA is extracted from blood, hair follicles or semen.
2. **Fragmentation** – the DNA is cut into fragments using enzymes called restriction enzymes.
3. **Separation** – the DNA sections are separated using a technique called electrophoresis.
4. **Comparison** – the DNA fingerprint is analysed by comparing it with a reference sample, e.g. blood taken from the crime scene.

Molecules of Life

Enzymes

Enzymes are proteins which act as biological catalysts. They speed up chemical reactions, including those that take place in living cells, e.g. respiration, photosynthesis and protein synthesis. Enzymes are highly specific; each one will only speed up a particular reaction.

Changing temperature and pH will affect the rate of a reaction catalysed by an enzyme.

Enzyme Activity and Temperature

The graph below shows the effect of temperature on enzyme activity:

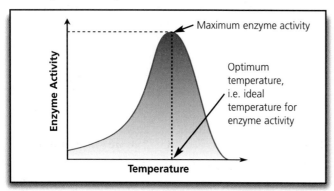

A rise in temperature increases the number of collisions between reactants and enzymes, and will increase the enzyme activity until the optimum temperature is reached. Temperatures above the optimum permanently damage the enzyme molecules, decreasing or stopping enzyme activity.

Different enzymes have different optimum temperatures. The ones in your body work best at about 37°C.

Enzyme Activity and pH

The graph below shows how changes in pH affect enzyme activity.

There is an optimum pH at which the enzyme works best. As the pH increases or decreases, the enzyme becomes less and less effective.

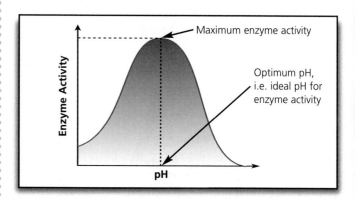

The optimum pH of different enzymes can vary considerably. For example…

- the enzyme in human saliva works best at about pH 7.3
- the enzyme pepsin (in the stomach) needs very acidic conditions in order to work well.

The Lock and Key Mechanism

Each enzyme has a different number and sequence of amino acids. This gives it a unique 3D shape, which includes an active site that only a specific reactant can fit into (like a key in a lock).

Enzyme molecules are denatured by high temperature and extreme pH; the bonds in the protein break and the shape of its active site is changed irreversibly, so the lock and key mechanism no longer works.

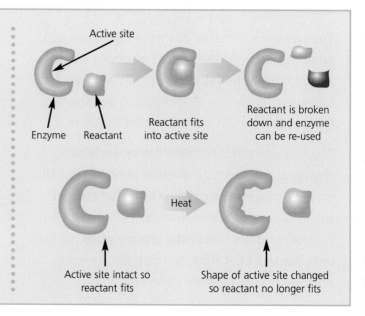

Diffusion

Diffusion

The cell membrane controls which substances enter and leave the cell. Living cells need to obtain oxygen, glucose, water and minerals from their surroundings and get rid of waste products, such as carbon dioxide. These substances pass through the cell membrane by **diffusion**.

Diffusion is the movement of a substance **from a region of high concentration to a region of low concentration**.

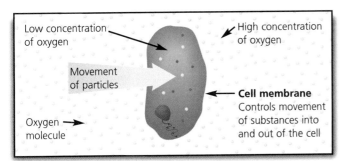

There is a low concentration of oxygen inside the cell because supplies are constantly being used up in respiration; there is a high concentration outside the cell because oxygen is constantly being replaced.

Particles move about in lots of different directions. This is called **random movement**. Diffusion is the net (overall) movement of particles from an area of high concentration to an area of low concentration.

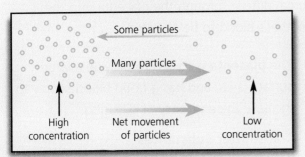

The rate of diffusion is increased when…
- the surface area of the cell membrane is greater
- there is a greater difference between concentrations (a steeper gradient)
- the particles have a shorter distance to travel.

Diffusion in Plants

During the day, carbon dioxide (CO_2) diffuses into plants through the stomata (tiny pores) on the bottom of their leaves. The CO_2 molecules move from a high concentration outside the leaf to a low concentration inside the leaf, where CO_2 is being used up in photosynthesis. Oxygen (O_2), which is a product of photosynthesis, diffuses in the opposite direction.

Magnified Cross-section of Leaf

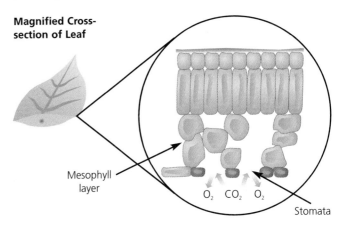

The diffusion of CO_2 and O_2 changes direction at night when photosynthesis stops.

Water is lost from plant leaves by evaporation. It diffuses out of cells into spaces in the spongy mesophyll layer (shown above). From there it passes out of the leaf and evaporates into the atmosphere.

Magnified View of Underside of Leaf

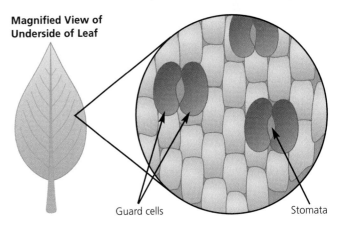

The stomata on the underside of leaves are a special adaptation which open in order to help increase the rate of diffusion of carbon dioxide and oxygen. They can also close to prevent excessive water loss in drought conditions.

Diffusion

Diffusion in Animals

Gaseous Exchange

Carbon dioxide is a waste product of respiration. It diffuses from body tissues into the blood to be carried to the lungs and is then expelled from the body.

In the lungs, carbon dioxide diffuses from the blood into alveoli, and oxygen (from the air) diffuses from the alveoli into the blood. This process is called **gaseous exchange**.

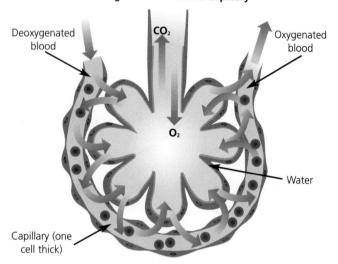

A Single Alveolus and a Capillary

Deoxygenated blood

CO_2

Oxygenated blood

O_2

Water

Capillary (one cell thick)

Blood leaving the alveoli in the lungs is rich in oxygen. It returns to the heart to be pumped around the body. As it travels around the body, oxygen diffuses out of the blood into the tissues.

(HT) The **alveoli** are specially adapted for efficient gaseous exchange: they have a massive surface area, a moist permeable surface which is only one cell thick, and a very good blood supply.

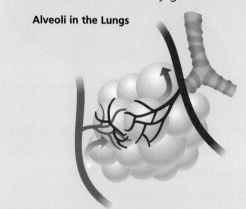

Alveoli in the Lungs

Absorption of Digested Food

In the intestine, large and insoluble food molecules are digested into smaller, soluble molecules (glucose, amino acids, fatty acids and glycerol), which diffuse into the blood. The blood carries them to the body tissues where they diffuse into cells.

(HT) The **small intestine** is well-adapted for absorbing food: it is very long, has a permeable surface, and has a good blood supply to remove the absorbed food quickly.

The inner surface of the small intestine is folded into **villi**, and the villi have tiny folds in their cell membranes called microvilli. The microvilli increase the surface area of the small intestine for better absorption.

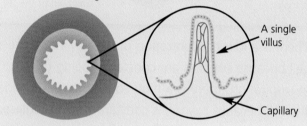

Villi Lining the Wall of the Small Intestine

A single villus

Capillary

The Developing Foetus

A growing foetus inside the uterus has no direct access to food or oxygen. It must receive oxygen, food and water from the mother's blood via the placenta. Carbon dioxide and other waste products (urea) diffuse through the placenta into the mother's blood to be excreted.

(HT) The **placenta** is folded to provide a large surface area, and has a good blood supply to increase the efficiency of diffusion.

Transmitter Substances

There is a very small gap between nerve cells, called a **synapse**. An electrical nerve impulse has to be able to cross this gap to travel from one nerve cell to the next. When an impulse reaches the synapse, a chemical transmitter is released. It crosses the gap between cells by diffusion, carrying the nerve impulse across.

The Blood

Blood transports food and oxygen to cells and removes waste products from the cells. It also forms part of the body's defence mechanism. It has four components:

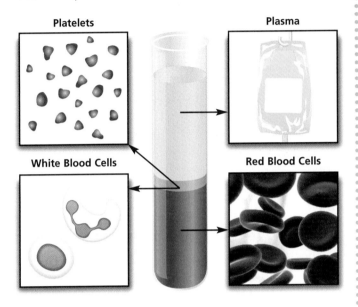

Platelets

Plasma

White Blood Cells

Red Blood Cells

Platelets are tiny pieces of cell, which have no nucleus. They clump together when a blood vessel becomes damaged and form a meshwork of fibres to produce a clot.

Plasma is a straw-coloured liquid which transports…
- carbon dioxide from the cells to the lungs
- glucose from the small intestine to the cells
- waste products (e.g. urea) from the liver to the kidneys
- hormones to the target organs
- antibodies to fight disease.

White blood cells protect the body against disease: some have a flexible shape, which enables them to engulf invading microorganisms; others produce antibodies to attack them.

Red blood cells transport oxygen from the lungs to the tissues. They are small and flexible, so they can pass through narrow blood vessels. They have no nucleus, so they can be packed with haemoglobin (the red pigment that carries oxygen). The shape of the cells increases their surface area for transferring oxygen.

HT The small size and biconcave shape of red blood cells gives them a large surface area in relation to their volume for transferring oxygen. When the cells reach the lungs, oxygen diffuses from the lungs into the blood. The haemoglobin molecules in the red blood cells bind with the oxygen to form oxyhaemoglobin.

$$\text{Haemoglobin} + \text{Oxygen} \longrightarrow \text{Oxyhaemoglobin}$$

The blood is then pumped around the body to the tissues, where the reverse reaction takes place. This releases the oxygen so that it can diffuse into the cells.

The Circulatory System

The **heart** pumps blood around the body in the blood vessels, transporting materials to and from the tissues:
- **arteries** transport blood away from the heart
- **veins** transport blood towards the heart
- **capillaries** are involved in exchanging materials with the tissues.

The human circulatory system is a double circulatory system; it consists of two loops:
- one which carries blood from the heart to the lungs, and then back to the heart
- one which carries blood from the heart to all other parts of the body, and then back to the heart.

Blood pumped out of the heart into the arteries is under much higher pressure than the blood returning to the heart in the veins.

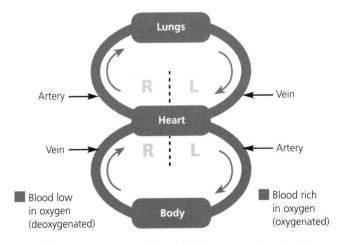

Lungs

Artery — R | L — Vein

Heart

Vein — R | L — Artery

Body

■ Blood low in oxygen (deoxygenated)

■ Blood rich in oxygen (oxygenated)

Keep it Moving

More on the Circulatory System

The advantage of a double circulatory system (common to all mammals) is that blood is pumped to the body at a higher pressure than it is pumped to the lungs, producing a much greater rate of flow to the body tissues.

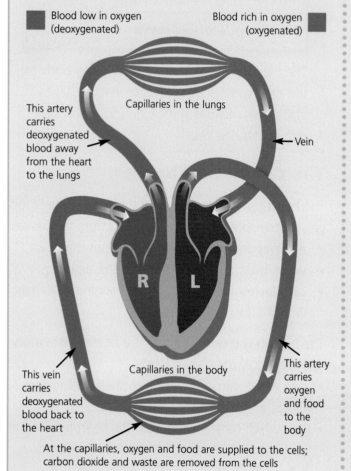

Blood low in oxygen (deoxygenated)

Blood rich in oxygen (oxygenated)

Capillaries in the lungs

This artery carries deoxygenated blood away from the heart to the lungs

Vein

R   L

This vein carries deoxygenated blood back to the heart

Capillaries in the body

This artery carries oxygen and food to the body

At the capillaries, oxygen and food are supplied to the cells; carbon dioxide and waste are removed from the cells

Arteries have a thick wall made of elastic muscle fibres to cope with the high pressure. The lumen (space inside) is small compared to the thickness of the walls. There are no valves.

Veins have thinner walls made of muscle fibres that are less elastic. The lumen is much bigger compared to the thickness of the walls and there are valves to prevent the backflow of blood.

Artery   Vein

Capillaries are narrow vessels with walls that are just one cell thick. These microscopic vessels connect arteries to veins. They are the only blood vessels that have permeable walls, to allow the exchange of substances between cells and blood.

A Working Muscle Cell

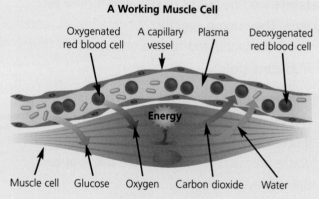

Oxygenated red blood cell   A capillary vessel   Plasma   Deoxygenated red blood cell

Energy

Muscle cell   Glucose   Oxygen   Carbon dioxide   Water

The Heart

Most of the wall of the heart is made of muscle. It has four chambers. The lower chambers, called **ventricles**, are large and muscular because they need to contract to pump blood out of the heart. The right ventricle pumps blood to the lungs. The left ventricle is more muscular because it has to pump blood around the whole body. The upper chambers, called **atria**, are smaller and less muscular. They receive blood coming back to the heart through the veins. Valves in the heart make sure that the blood flows in the right direction (not backwards).

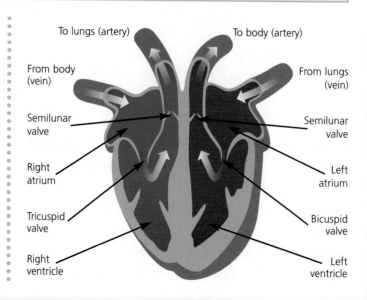

To lungs (artery)   To body (artery)

From body (vein)   From lungs (vein)

Semilunar valve   Semilunar valve

Right atrium   Left atrium

Tricuspid valve   Bicuspid valve

Right ventricle   Left ventricle

Coronary Heart Disease

Meat, eggs and dairy products contain a lot of saturated fat and **cholesterol**. Excess cholesterol from food can be deposited in the walls of the arteries. This forms a hard plaque which bulges into the lumen, restricting or blocking blood flow through the artery.

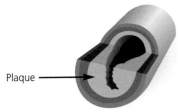

Plaque

The **coronary artery** supplies essential glucose and oxygen to the heart muscle. If it becomes blocked the heart muscle around it can die, causing a **heart attack**.

Mending the Heart

A normal heart contracts and relaxes regularly by itself. But a diseased heart can start to beat slowly or irregularly. If this happens, a **pacemaker** can be implanted into the chest to stimulate the heart so that it beats in a regular rhythm.

Pacemakers are powered by small batteries, which need to be replaced every two years. This requires a small operation.

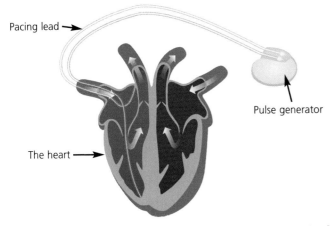

Pacing lead →

Pulse generator

The heart →

The heart valves can also be replaced with **mechanical** or **biological valves** if they become weak. Mechanical valves are more durable but they can cause blood clots, so patients must take anticoagulants (blood thinning drugs) for the rest of their lives. There are dangers: the body's immune system can reject implants and the surrounding tissues may die.

Heart Transplants

A severely diseased heart can be replaced in a **heart transplant**. During the operation, the patient has to be kept alive on a heart–lung machine.

There are some problems with heart transplants:
* there is a shortage of donor hearts so the waiting list is long (not everyone is willing to sign up as an organ donor)
* the donor heart has to be the right size and age for the patient
* the donor and the patient must have the same blood and tissue type so that the patient's body does not reject the new heart
* the patient has to take immunosuppressant drugs for the rest of their life to prevent their immune system from destroying the new heart.

The table below lists the factors that need to be considered when deciding whether a patient needs a heart transplant, or a pacemaker or replacement valves fitted.

Heart Transplant

* Major, expensive operation.
* Replacement heart must come from a dead donor.
* Long waiting time for suitable donor (must be right age, size, etc.).
* Need to take immunosuppressants for the rest of their life.

Heart Pacemaker or Valve Replacement

* Relatively minor operation.
* No human donor needed.
* Valves can be artificial (mechanical) devices or can come from cow or pig hearts.
* Pacemakers are mechanical devices.
* Shorter waiting time than for a donor heart.
* Need to take anticoagulants for the rest of their life.

Divide and Rule

Single-Cell and Multi-Cell Organisms

Single-cell organisms (e.g. amoeba) are very small and have to rely on diffusion to obtain glucose and oxygen, and to remove waste products.

Multi-cell organisms (e.g. humans) are much larger and more complex. They have specialised organs to carry out functions like gas exchange and digestion. These organs can then efficiently supply other cells in the body with glucose and oxygen.

HT One large cell (see **1**) has a smaller surface area to volume ratio than several smaller ones (see **2**). Diffusion of substances in and out of the larger cell will therefore be much slower.

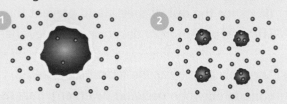

Cell Division

In mammals, body cells are **diploid**, which means they contain two sets of chromosomes.

Mitosis is the process by which a diploid cell divides to produce two more diploid cells. It produces new cells…

- for **growth**
- to **repair** damaged tissue
- to **replace** old cells.

HT During mitosis, the chromosomes in the cell are copied to produce two cells which are genetically identical.

Parental cell with two pairs of chromosomes.

Each chromosome replicates itself.

The replicas separate from the originals and move to opposite poles of the cell. The cell then divides for the only time.

Each 'daughter' cell has the same number of chromosomes as the parental cell and contains the same genes as the parental cell.

Meiosis is another type of cell division, which occurs in the testes and ovaries. The cells in these organs divide to produce gametes (sex cells: eggs and sperm) for sexual reproduction. Gametes are **haploid** cells, which means they have only one set of chromosomes.

HT During meiosis, a diploid cell divides twice to produce four haploid cells, with genetically different sets of chromosomes.

Diploid cell (in this example, two sets of chromosomes).

Each chromosome replicates itself.

Pairs of chromosomes part company and move to opposite poles with their replicas.

Cell divides for the first time.

Copies now separate and the second cell division takes place.

Four haploid cells (gametes), each with half the number of chromosomes of the parental cell.

Fertilisation

Fertilisation occurs during sexual reproduction. Two gametes (an egg and a sperm) fuse together to form a diploid zygote (fertilised egg), with two sets of chromosomes.

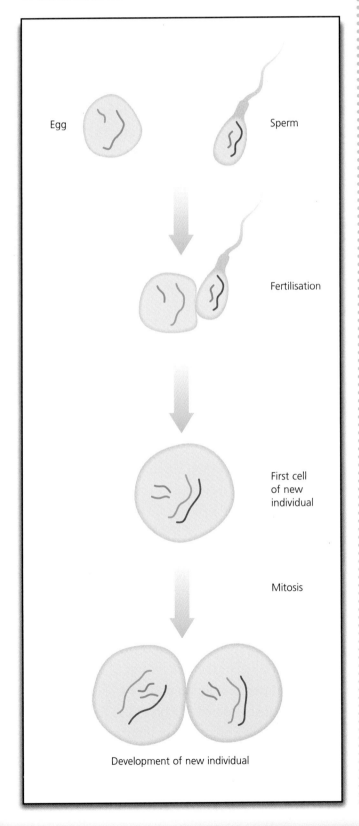

Egg

Sperm

Fertilisation

First cell of new individual

Mitosis

Development of new individual

Gametes

Gametes are specialised haploid cells. This means they have only one set of each chromosome.

Ovum (Egg Cell)

An ovum is a large cell, because it needs to contain massive food reserves for the developing embryo. The nucleus contains one set of genes from the mother.

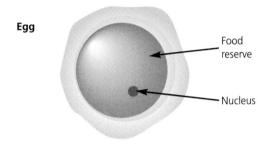

Egg

Food reserve

Nucleus

Sperm Cell

A sperm is a tiny cell with a short life span. It is amazingly mobile because of its tail, and contains many mitochondria to supply the energy needed for swimming. On contact with the egg, its acrosome (a cap-like structure on the sperm's 'head') bursts. This releases enzymes that digest the egg cell's membrane, allowing the sperm nucleus, containing one set of genes from the father, to enter.

Sperm are produced and released in vast numbers to increase the chance of fertilisation occurring.

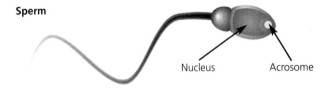

Sperm

Nucleus

Acrosome

N.B. Egg and sperm images are not to scale.

Variation Through Sexual Reproduction

Sexual reproduction promotes variation because…
- the gametes are produced by meiosis, which 'shuffles' the genes
- gametes fuse randomly, with one of each pair of alleles for a gene coming from each parent
- the alleles in a pair may be the same or different, producing different characteristics.

Growing Up

Plant Cells

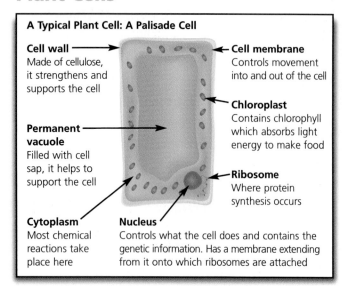

A Typical Plant Cell: A Palisade Cell

Cell wall
Made of cellulose, it strengthens and supports the cell

Cell membrane
Controls movement into and out of the cell

Chloroplast
Contains chlorophyll which absorbs light energy to make food

Permanent vacuole
Filled with cell sap, it helps to support the cell

Ribosome
Where protein synthesis occurs

Cytoplasm
Most chemical reactions take place here

Nucleus
Controls what the cell does and contains the genetic information. Has a membrane extending from it onto which ribosomes are attached

- Plant and animal cells contain a nucleus, cell membrane, mitochondria and cytoplasm.
- Only plant cells contain chloroplasts, a cellulose cell wall and a vacuole.

To see the parts of a plant cell, use tweezers to peel a thin layer of skin tissue from an onion. Place the onion tissue onto a microscope slide on top of a drop of distilled water. Add a drop of distilled water and a drop of iodine to the tissue and carefully cover the slide. You should be able to see the parts of an onion cell at x100 magnification.

Growth

Animals grow by increasing the number of cells. The cells specialise or **differentiate** into different types of cell at an early stage to form tissues and organs. An animal will eventually stop growing, whereas, given the right conditions, many plants can grow continuously by cell division and by enlarging the size of their cells.

Stem Cells

Stem cells are undifferentiated animal cells, which can specialise and develop into different types of cells, tissues and organs. Stem cells found in embryos can specialise into any type of cell. Stem cells found in some adult tissues such as bone marrow can only specialise into a limited variety of cells, e.g. blood or bone cells.

More About Growth

Cell enlargement is the main method by which plants gain height; cells in the stem absorb water and elongate.

Cell division is mainly restricted to the tips of the roots and shoots. The cells specialise into xylem, phloem and a variety of other types of cell.

Unlike animal cells, plant cells retain the ability to differentiate or specialise throughout their lives. If you take cuttings from a section of stem, some of the cells will be able to turn into root cells.

More About Stem Cells

There are a lot of potential uses for stem cells. Scientists believe they could be useful for…

- **research** – to investigate how cell division goes wrong in diseases like cancer
- **drug testing** – to test the safety of new medicines
- **transplants** – to replace damaged or diseased cells, or grow new organs for transplantation.

In order to carry out research, scientists need to obtain embryos in large numbers and to grow the stem cells in the laboratory. At the moment the embryos used come from **IVF** (*in vitro* fertilisation) treatments for infertile couples. Only a few of the embryos produced by IVF treatment are implanted back into the woman, so scientists can use the remaining ones with the couple's consent.

There are opposing views about obtaining embryos for stem cell research. One side of the argument is that the embryos left over from IVF treatment would be destroyed in any case, so stem cell research is a good use for them. The other viewpoint is that embryos have the potential to become a human being, so it is wrong to experiment on them.

Gestation

The larger and more complex an organism is, the longer the **gestation period** (pregnancy) will be. For example, human gestation lasts for 266 days on average, compared to mouse gestation, which lasts for 19 days, and killer whale gestation, which lasts for 517 days.

A human foetus in the uterus grows very quickly. Different body parts develop at different rates. The head and brain grow rapidly at first to coordinate the complex growth of the rest of the body.

Stages of Development in the Womb

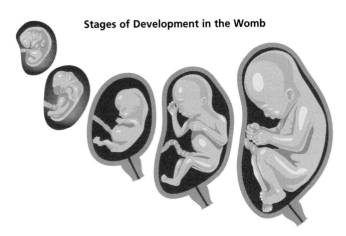

Human Growth

There are five main stages to human growth:
1. infancy
2. childhood
3. adolescence (puberty)
4. maturity (adulthood)
5. old age.

Baby Growth

A human baby's growth is carefully monitored for the first few years; the **weight** and **head circumference** are measured regularly, to check that they are normal for a child of that age.

> **HT** Head circumference is an indication of whether the brain is growing normally. Weight (proportional to length) reveals if the baby is getting enough food to grow healthily.

Example

The weight and head circumference of a baby were measured once a month for a year. The measurements are plotted on the graphs below.

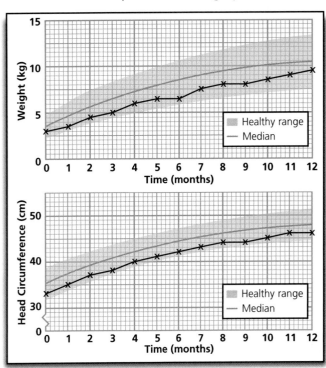

By comparing the baby's measurements to the normal range of weight and head circumference, we can see that the baby's measurements were towards the lower end of healthy weight and head circumference.

Childhood and Adolescent Growth

We grow fastest during infancy and early childhood, and have another growth spurt in adolescence when we hit puberty. As adults (18 and over) we grow very little, if at all. The graph below shows how many centimetres boys and girls grow on average each year for the first 20 years of their life.

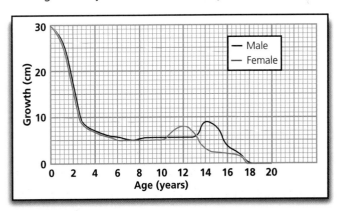

Controlling Plant Growth

Plant Hormones

Plant hormones (auxins) are chemicals that control the **growth** of shoots and roots, **flowering**, and the **ripening** of fruits. The different hormones move through the plant in solution and affect its growth by responding to **gravity (geotropism)** and **light (phototropism)**.

Shoots grow towards light (positive phototropism) and against gravity (negative geotropism).

Roots grow away from light (negative phototropism) and in the direction of gravity (positive geotropism).

The diagram below shows an experiment that can be carried out to show that shoots grow towards light. A hole is cut out of the side of two boxes to enable light to enter. Three cuttings of a plant are put in one of the boxes (see diagram **1**). Another three cuttings are put in the other box, but the tips of the shoots are covered with foil (see diagram **2**). The normal shoot tips detect the light and grow towards it. However, the shoots covered in foil cannot detect the light so they grow straight up.

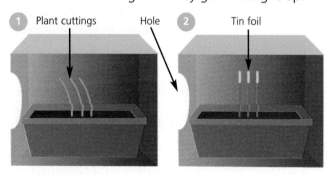

Commercial Uses of Hormones

Plant hormones can be used in agriculture to speed up or slow down plant growth:

- **rooting powder** – consists of a hormone which encourages the growth of roots in stem cuttings so lots of plants can be obtained from one plant
- **fruit-ripening hormone** – causes fruit to ripen (fruits are sometimes harvested whilst still under-ripe and sprayed with the hormone during transportation so that they are ripe when they reach the shops)

- **selective weedkillers** – hormones in the weedkiller disrupt the growth patterns of their target plants without harming other plants
- **control of dormancy** – hormones can be used to speed up or slow down plant growth and bud development, allowing the farmer to control dormancy and get the best price at market.

Gravity

Hormones in solution travel down towards the lower side of shoots and roots:
- in the shoots, the hormones increase growth in the lower region, which makes the shoot bend upwards
- in the roots, the hormones slow down growth in the lower region, which makes the root bend downwards.

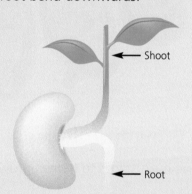

Light

Auxin is made in the shoot tip. Its distribution through the plant is determined by light. When light shines on a shoot, the hormones in direct sunlight are destroyed. The hormones on the shaded side continue to function, causing the cells to elongate. This makes the shoot bend towards the light.

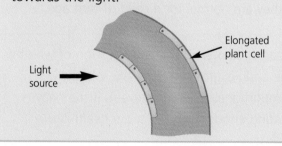

Mutations

Remember that…
- changes to genes happen randomly and spontaneously due to mutations
- the rate of mutation is increased by environmental factors such as radiation or chemicals
- most mutations are harmful but occasionally a beneficial mutation occurs.

Selective Breeding

Farmers have used the principles of selective breeding for hundreds of years by keeping the best animals and plants for breeding and taking the rest to market. The same is true for dog breeders who have systematically selected animals that show the desired characteristics and bred them, e.g. the spottiest dogs have been bred through the generations, to eventually get Dalmations.

Development of Modern Vegetables

The diagram below illustrates how three of our modern vegetables have come from a single ancestor by selective breeding.

N.B. It can take many, many generations to get the desired results.

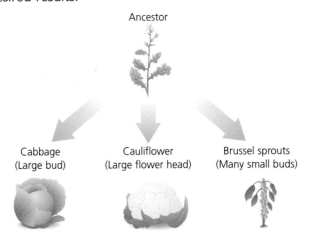

Ancestor

Cabbage (Large bud) Cauliflower (Large flower head) Brussel sprouts (Many small buds)

Development of Modern Cattle

Selective breeding can contribute to improved yields in cattle, for example…
- **quantity of milk** – years of selecting and breeding cattle that produce larger than average quantities of milk has produced herds of cows that produce high volumes of milk daily
- **quality of milk** – as a result of selective breeding, Jersey cows produce milk that is rich and creamy and can therefore be sold at a higher price
- **beef production** – the characteristics of the Hereford and Angus varieties have been selected over the past 200 years or more. They include hardiness, early maturity, high numbers of offspring, and the swift, efficient conversion of grass into body mass (meat).

Similarly, improved yields in crops have been obtained by selective breeding.

More on Mutations

Mutations change the base sequence of DNA, which alters or prevents the synthesis of the protein that the gene normally codes for.

Advantages and Disadvantages of Selective Breeding

Selective breeding results in an organism with the 'right' characteristics for a particular function. In farming and horticulture it is a more efficient and economically viable process than natural selection.

However, intensive selective breeding reduces the gene pool; the number of alleles in the population decreases so there is less variation. This reduces the species' ability to respond to environmental change and limits the opportunities for further selective breeding. It can also lead to an accumulation of harmful recessive characteristics (in-breeding).

New Genes for Old

Genetic Engineering

Because all living organisms use the same basic genetic code (DNA), genes can be transferred from one organism to another in order to deliberately change the recipient's characteristics. This process is called **genetic engineering** or **genetic modification (GM)**.

Altering the genetic make-up of an organism can be done for many reasons, for example…

- **to improve resistance to herbicides,** e.g. soya plants are genetically modified by inserting a gene that makes them resistant to a herbicide. When the crop fields are sprayed with the herbicide only the weeds die, leaving the soya plants without competition so they can grow better

- **to improve the quality of food,** e.g. the genes responsible for producing beta-carotene (which is converted into vitamin A in humans) are transferred from carrots to rice plants. People whose diets lack vitamin A can then get beta-carotene from rice

- **to produce a substance you require,** e.g. the gene for human insulin can be inserted into bacteria to make insulin on a large scale to treat diabetes.

Genetic engineering allows organisms with new features to be produced. It can also be used to make biochemical processes cheaper and more efficient. However, the transplanted genes may have unexpected harmful effects.

Producing Insulin

The following method is used to produce insulin:

1. The human gene for insulin production is identified. It is removed using a special enzyme, called a restriction enzyme, which cuts through the DNA strands in precise places.
2. Another restriction enzyme is used to cut open a ring of bacterial DNA (**a plasmid**). Other enzymes are then used to **insert** the section of human DNA into the plasmid.
3. The plasmid is reinserted into a bacterium which starts to divide rapidly. As it divides it **replicates** the plasmid.
4. The bacteria are cultivated on a large scale in vats called **fermenters**. Each bacteria carries the instructions to make insulin. When the bacteria then make the protein, commercial quantities of insulin are produced.

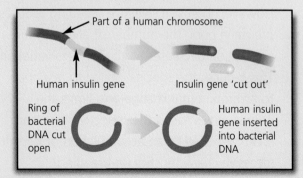

Part of a human chromosome

Human insulin gene   Insulin gene 'cut out'

Ring of bacterial DNA cut open   Human insulin gene inserted into bacterial DNA

Ethical Considerations

There are many benefits of genetic engineering, such as producing disease-resistant crops and higher yields, and potentially faulty genes could be replaced to reduce certain diseases. However, there are concerns that…

- genetically modified plants may cross-breed with wild plants and release their new genes into the environment
- GM foods may not be safe to eat in the long term
- rather than just replacing 'faulty' genes, parents may want to modify or engineer the genetic make-up of their child ('designer babies').

Currently, genetic screening takes place in certain circumstances, but there is a fear that screening could become more widespread and…

- unborn children could be genetically screened and aborted if their genetic make-up is 'faulty'
- insurance companies could genetically screen applicants and refuse to insure people who have an increased risk of illness, preventing them from being able to drive a car or buy a home.

More of the Same

Asexual Reproduction in Plants

Plants can reproduce asexually (i.e. without a partner) and many do so naturally. In asexual reproduction, a cell divides by mitosis (see p.12) to produce two identical cells; each new cell continues to divide and develop to produce genetically identical individuals or **clones**.

The spider plant, strawberry plant and potato plant all reproduce in this way.

Spider Plant Stolons

Stolon – a rooting side branch

New individual established

New individual now independent

Taking Cuttings

When a gardener has a plant with all the desired characteristics, he may choose to produce lots of them by taking stem, leaf or root cuttings. The cuttings are grown in a damp atmosphere until roots develop.

Taking a Cutting

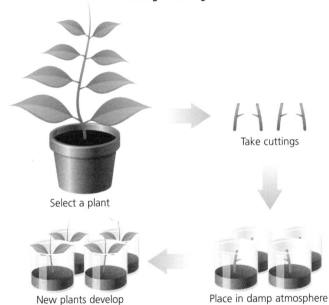

Select a plant

Take cuttings

Place in damp atmosphere

New plants develop

Commercial Cloning of Plants

In modern horticulture, prize plant specimens are cloned to produce thousands more, which can be sold. The advantages and disadvantages of this process are listed in the following table.

Advantages

- You can be sure of the characteristics of the offspring, as they will all be genetically identical to the parent.
- It is possible to mass produce large numbers of plants, which may have been more difficult, or taken more time, to grow from seed.

Disadvantages

- If the plants become susceptible to disease or sensitive to a change in the environment, all of the plants will be affected.
- The reduction in genetic variation reduces the potential for further selective breeding.

Cloning by Tissue Culture

To produce offspring that are genetically identical to the parent plant and to each other, horticulturalists follow this method:

1. Select a parent plant with the characteristics that you want.
2. Scrape off a few cells into several beakers containing nutrients and hormones.
3. A week or two later there will be lots and lots of genetically identical plantlets growing. The same can be done to these.

This whole process must be aseptic (i.e. carried out in the absence of harmful bacteria), otherwise the new plants will rot.

Remember, many older plant cells are still able to differentiate or specialise, whereas animal cells lose this ability. This means that cloning plants is easier than cloning animals.

More of the Same

Cloning Animals

Identical twins are naturally occurring clones in animals. A single fertilised egg forms an embryo which splits into two at an early stage. The two individuals develop from the same fertilised egg and have identical genetic make-up.

Artificial cloning of animals is now used quite widely. The most famous animal clone is Dolly the sheep – the first mammal to be successfully cloned from an adult body cell.

A cloning technique called **embryo transplantation** is now commonly used in cattle breeding (see diagram alongside):

1 Sperm is collected from a bull with desirable characteristics.

2 A selected cow is artificially inseminated with the bull's sperm.

3 The fertilised egg develops into an embryo which is removed from the cow at an early stage.

4 In the laboratory, the embryo is split to form several clones.

5 Each clone is transplanted into a cow who will be the surrogate mother to the new calf.

Animal Organ Donors

There is a shortage of human organ donors for transplants. One possible solution is to use animal organs. Animal organs would normally be rejected and destroyed by the human immune system. However, animal embryos could potentially be genetically modified so that they will not be rejected. They could then be cloned to produce a ready supply of identical organ donors.

Human Cloning

It is possible to clone human embryos in the same way that animals are cloned. This technique could be used to provide stem cells for medical purposes. However, if the embryos were allowed to develop they would produce human clones, so this type of research is currently illegal.

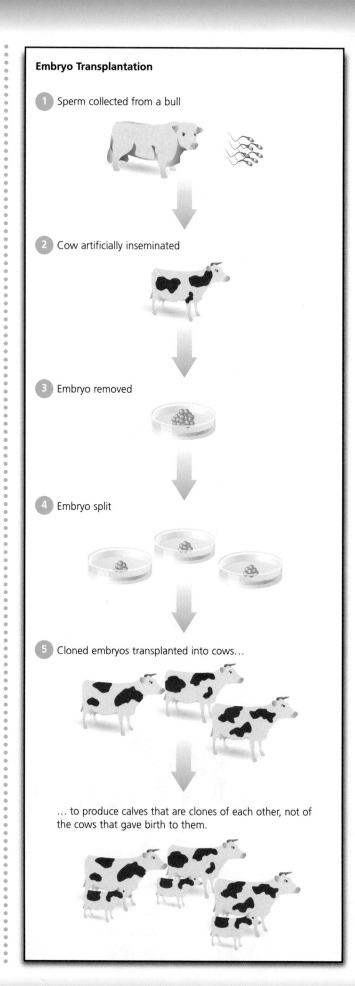

Embryo Transplantation

1 Sperm collected from a bull

2 Cow artificially inseminated

3 Embryo removed

4 Embryo split

5 Cloned embryos transplanted into cows…

… to produce calves that are clones of each other, not of the cows that gave birth to them.

Adult Cell Cloning

The following method was used to produce a cloned sheep (Dolly):

1. A nucleus was taken from an udder cell of an adult sheep, and the nucleus was removed from an egg cell of a female sheep.
2. The nucleus from the udder cell was then inserted into the empty egg cell.
3. The resulting embryo was placed into the uterus of a surrogate mother sheep.
4. The embryo developed into a foetus and was born as normal. The offspring produced (Dolly) was a clone of the sheep which the nucleus came from.

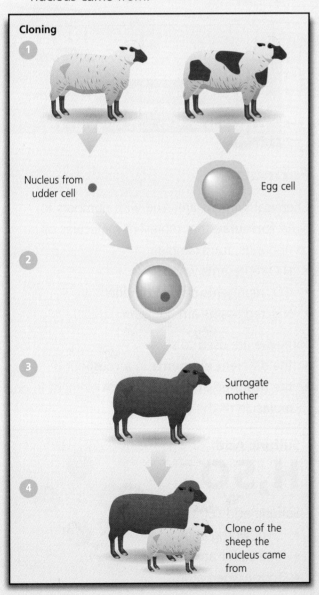

Cloning

1
Nucleus from udder cell
Egg cell
2
3
Surrogate mother
4
Clone of the sheep the nucleus came from

Benefits and Risks of Cloning

There are benefits and risks associated with cloning technology:

Benefits
• Genetically identical cloned animals will all have the same characteristics. • It is possible for a farmer to choose the sex and timing of birth. • Top-quality bulls and cows can be kept for egg and sperm donation, whilst other animals can be used to carry and give birth to the young.

Risks
• Just like selective breeding, cloning reduces genetic variation in the herd. • Animals are in-bred so there is the potential for accumulating inherited disease. • There are some animal welfare concerns that cloned animals may not be as healthy or live as long as 'normal' animals.

More on Animal Organ Donors

Animal organ donors could solve the problem of waiting lists for human transplants. But there are concerns that infections might be passed from animals to humans and there are ethical issues concerning animal welfare and rights.

More on Human Cloning

There are major concerns about cloning humans:
- the cloning process is very unreliable – the vast majority of cloned embryos do not survive
- cloned animals seem to have a limited life span and die early
- the effect of cloning on a human's mental and emotional development is not known.

Fundamental Chemical Concepts

For modules C3 and C4, you need to have a good understanding of the following concepts (ideas).

Atoms

All substances are made up of **atoms**. Atoms contain three types of particles:

- **protons**
- **neutrons** (except hydrogen)
- **electrons**.

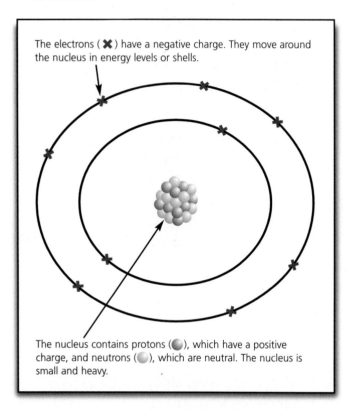

The electrons (✖) have a negative charge. They move around the nucleus in energy levels or shells.

The nucleus contains protons (⚪), which have a positive charge, and neutrons (⚪), which are neutral. The nucleus is small and heavy.

Elements and Compounds

Elements are substances made up of just **one** type of atom.

Compounds are substances formed from the atoms of **two** or more elements, which have been **joined** together by a chemical bond.

There are two ways they can do this:

- **covalent bonding** – two atoms share a pair of electrons. (The atoms in molecules are held together by covalent bonds.)
- **ionic bonding** – atoms turn into ions (become charged by losing or gaining electrons) and then the positive ions attract the negative ions.

Chemical Reactions

In a **chemical reaction** the substances that you start with are called **reactants**. During the reaction, the atoms in the reactants are rearranged in some way to form new substances called **products**. No atoms are lost or gained during the reaction.

Chemical Symbols

Each element is represented by a different **chemical symbol**, for example…

- Fe represents iron
- Na represents sodium.

These symbols are all arranged in **periods** (rows) and **groups** (columns) in the **periodic table**.

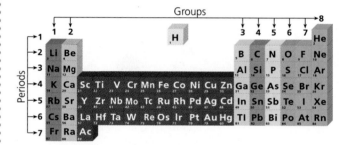

Formulae

Chemical symbols are used with numbers to write **formulae** that represent molecules of compounds, for example…

- H_2O represents water
- CO_2 represents carbon dioxide
- NH_3 represents ammonia.

Formulae are used to show…

- the different **elements** in a compound
- the **number of atoms** of each element in one molecule of the compound.

Sulfuric Acid

H_2SO_4

Sulfuric acid contains…

- two hydrogen atoms
- one sulfur atom
- four oxygen atoms.

If there are **brackets** around part of the formula, everything inside the brackets is multiplied by the number outside (see below).

Calcium Nitrate

$$2Ca(NO_3)_2$$

($NO_3)_2$ means 2 x NO_3, i.e. $NO_3 + NO_3$

The '2' in the chemical formula above tells us that there are two calcium nitrates.

Each calcium nitrate contains…
- one calcium atom
- two nitrogen atoms
- six oxygen atoms.

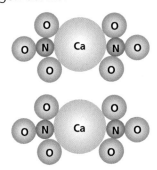

Displayed Formulae

A displayed formula is another way to show the composition of a molecule, e.g. ethanol, C_2H_5OH.

$$\begin{array}{c} \text{H} \quad \text{H} \\ | \quad | \\ \text{H} - \text{C} - \text{C} - \text{O} - \text{H} \\ | \quad | \\ \text{H} \quad \text{H} \end{array}$$

The displayed formula for an ethanol molecule (above) shows…
- the **different types of atom** in the molecule: carbon, hydrogen and oxygen
- the **number of each different type of atom**: one oxygen atom, two carbon atoms and six hydrogen atoms
- the **covalent bonds** between the atoms (shown by the line −).

You need to know the formulae for the following compounds:

Carbonates
- Copper (II) carbonate, $CuCO_3$
- Iron (II) carbonate, $FeCO_3$
- Manganese carbonate, $MnCO_3$
- Zinc carbonate, $ZnCO_3$

Chlorides
- Barium chloride, $BaCl_2$
- Magnesium chloride, $MgCl_2$
- Potassium chloride, KCl
- Sodium chloride, NaCl

Hydroxides
- Copper (II) hydroxide, $Cu(OH)_2$
- Iron (II) hydroxide, $Fe(OH)_2$
- Iron (III) hydroxide, $Fe(OH)_3$
- Lithium hydroxide, LiOH
- Potassium hydroxide, KOH
- Sodium hydroxide, NaOH

Oxides
- Aluminium oxide, Al_2O_3
- Copper (I!) oxide, CuO
- Iron (II) oxide, FeO
- Magnesium oxide, MgO
- Manganese oxide, MnO_2
- Sodium oxide, Na_2O
- Zinc oxide, ZnO

Others
- Carbon dioxide, CO_2
- Methane, CH_4
- Silver nitrate, $AgNO_3$
- Water, H_2O

Try to learn as many of the formulae in this book as you can – it will help you in your exams.

  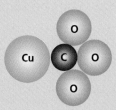

Fundamental Chemical Concepts

Equations

Chemists use **equations** to show what has happened during a **chemical reaction**. The **reactants** are on one side and the **products** are on the other. We know that no atoms are lost or gained during a chemical reaction, so the equation must be balanced: there must always be the same number of atoms of each element on both sides of the equation.

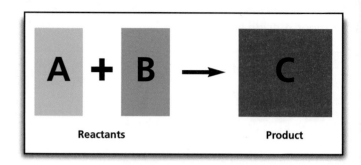

Balancing Equations

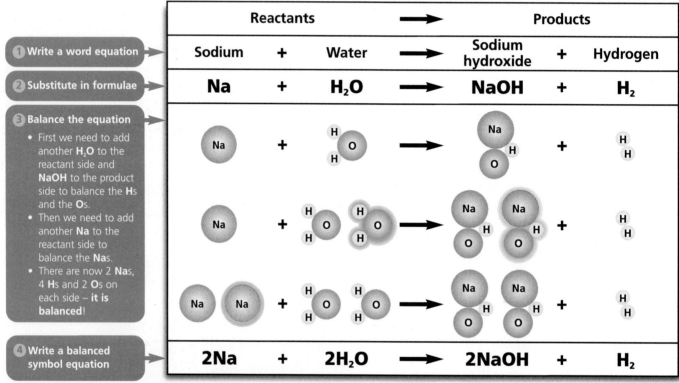

	Reactants			➡	Products		
① Write a word equation	Sodium	+	Water	➡	Sodium hydroxide	+	Hydrogen
② Substitute in formulae	Na	+	H_2O	➡	NaOH	+	H_2

③ **Balance the equation**
- First we need to add another H_2O to the reactant side and **NaOH** to the product side to balance the **H**s and the **O**s.
- Then we need to add another **Na** to the reactant side to balance the **Na**s.
- There are now 2 **Na**s, 4 **H**s and 2 **O**s on each side – **it is balanced!**

④ Write a balanced symbol equation

$$2Na + 2H_2O \longrightarrow 2NaOH + H_2$$

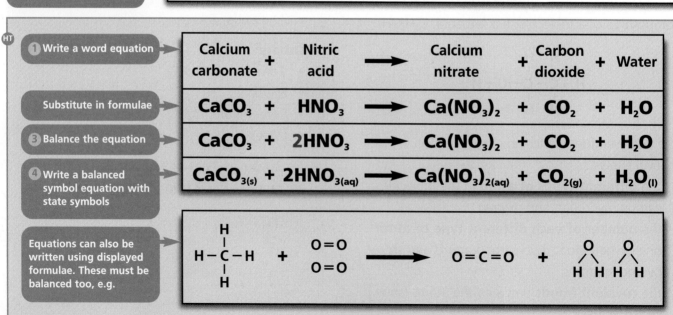

HT

① Write a word equation

Calcium carbonate	+	Nitric acid	➡	Calcium nitrate	+	Carbon dioxide	+ Water

Substitute in formulae

$$CaCO_3 + HNO_3 \longrightarrow Ca(NO_3)_2 + CO_2 + H_2O$$

③ Balance the equation

$$CaCO_3 + 2HNO_3 \longrightarrow Ca(NO_3)_2 + CO_2 + H_2O$$

④ Write a balanced symbol equation with state symbols

$$CaCO_{3(s)} + 2HNO_{3(aq)} \longrightarrow Ca(NO_3)_{2(aq)} + CO_{2(g)} + H_2O_{(l)}$$

Equations can also be written using displayed formulae. These must be balanced too, e.g.

What are Atoms Like?

Structure of an Atom

All substances are made up of **atoms**. All atoms have a central **nucleus**. The nucleus is positively charged because it is made up of **protons** which are positively charged and **neutrons** which are neutral. The nucleus is surrounded by negatively charged **electrons** arranged in shells. Overall, an atom has **no charge**.

> An atom has no overall charge because it has the same number of protons and electrons, so they cancel out each other's charges.

A Fluorine Atom

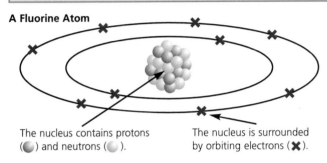

The nucleus contains protons ( ) and neutrons ( ).

The nucleus is surrounded by orbiting electrons (✗).

Atomic Particle		Relative Charge	Relative Mass
Proton		+1	1
Neutron		0	1
Electron	✗	-1	0.0005 (zero)

The relative masses and relative charges of atomic particles can be summarised in the following ways:
- a proton has the same mass as a neutron
- the mass of an electron is negligible, i.e. nearly nothing compared to a proton or neutron
- a substance that contains only one sort of atom is called an element.

Elements and Compounds

An **element** is a substance that cannot be broken down chemically and contains only one type of atom. There are about **100** different kinds of element and each one is made up of protons, neutrons and electrons.

A **compound** is a substance that contains at least two elements that are **chemically combined**. You can find out which elements make up a compound by looking at the compound's **formula** and identifying the elements from the periodic table, for example…
- sodium chloride (NaCl) contains the elements sodium (Na) and chlorine (Cl)
- potassium nitrate (KNO_3) contains the elements potassium (K), nitrogen (N) and oxygen (O).

Mass Number and Atomic Number

The numbers next to the elements in the periodic table tell us a lot, for example, the fluorine atom:

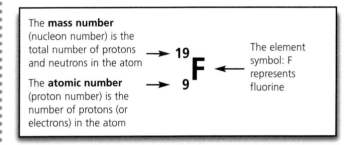

The **mass number** (nucleon number) is the total number of protons and neutrons in the atom

The **atomic number** (proton number) is the number of protons (or electrons) in the atom

$^{19}_{9}F$

The element symbol: F represents fluorine

The elements in the periodic table are arranged in order of ascending atomic number, starting with hydrogen (atomic number 1) at the top.

You can use the periodic table to find an element if you know its atomic number. Likewise, if you know where the element is in the periodic table you can find its atomic number.

Isotopes

All atoms of a particular element have the same number of protons. (Different numbers of protons indicate atoms of different elements.) However, some elements have varieties that have different numbers of neutrons; these are called **isotopes**. They are easy to spot because they have the same atomic number but a different mass number. For example, chlorine has two isotopes:

$^{35}_{17}Cl$

Mass number = 35
Atomic number = 17

$^{37}_{17}Cl$

Mass number = 37
Atomic number = 17

What are Atoms Like?

More on Mass Number, Atomic Number and Isotopes

As we have previously seen…

- the atomic number gives the number of protons, which is equal to the number of electrons because atoms have no overall charge
- the mass number is the total number of protons and neutrons in the atom.

$$\text{Number of neutrons} = \text{Mass number} - \text{Atomic number}$$

Table 1 (below) shows some common elements and how the number of protons, neutrons and electrons can be calculated from the atomic number and mass number.

In isotopes, the number of neutrons varies and this affects the mass number, e.g. carbon has three main isotopes (see Table 2 below).

N.B. Each isotope has the same number of protons and electrons, but a different number of neutrons.

Electron configuration tells us how the electrons are arranged around the nucleus in **shells**:

- The electrons in an atom occupy the lowest available shells.
- The first energy level or shell can only contain a maximum of 2 electrons.
- The shells after this can hold a maximum of 8 electrons.
- We write the electron configuration as a series of numbers, e.g. oxygen is 2, 6; aluminium is 2, 8, 3; and potassium is 2, 8, 8, 1.

Table 1

Chemical Symbol	Chemical Name	Number of Protons	Number of Electrons	Number of Neutrons
$^{1}_{1}\text{H}$	Hydrogen	1	1	0 (1 – 1 = 0)
$^{4}_{2}\text{He}$	Helium	2	2	2 (4 – 2 = 2)
$^{16}_{8}\text{O}$	Oxygen	8	8	8 (16 – 8 = 8)
$^{23}_{11}\text{Na}$	Sodium	11	11	12 (23 – 11 = 12)

Table 2

Isotope	Symbol	Mass Number	Atomic Number	Protons	Neutrons	Electrons
Carbon-12	$^{12}_{6}\text{C}$	12	6	6	6	6
Carbon-13	$^{13}_{6}\text{C}$	13	6	6	7	6
Carbon-14	$^{14}_{6}\text{C}$	14	6	6	8	6

The Modern Periodic Table – Electronic Structure of the First 20 Elements

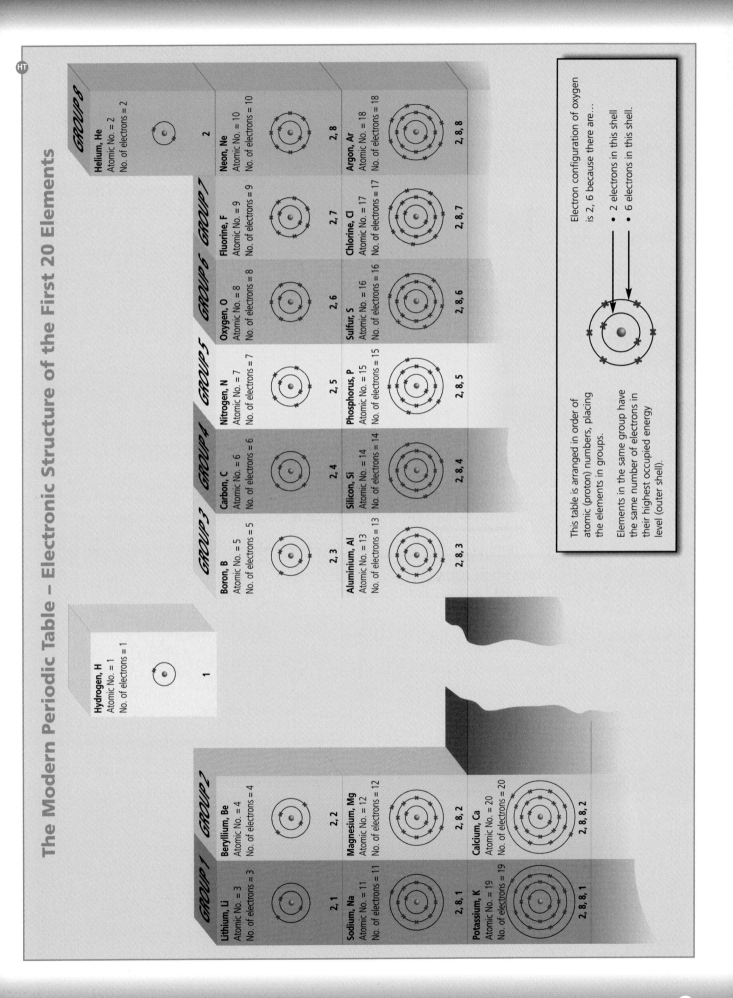

Hydrogen, H
Atomic No. = 1
No. of electrons = 1

1

GROUP 1

Lithium, Li
Atomic No. = 3
No. of electrons = 3

2, 1

Sodium, Na
Atomic No. = 11
No. of electrons = 11

2, 8, 1

Potassium, K
Atomic No. = 19
No. of electrons = 19

2, 8, 8, 1

GROUP 2

Beryllium, Be
Atomic No. = 4
No. of electrons = 4

2, 2

Magnesium, Mg
Atomic No. = 12
No. of electrons = 12

2, 8, 2

Calcium, Ca
Atomic No. = 20
No. of electrons = 20

2, 8, 8, 2

GROUP 3

Boron, B
Atomic No. = 5
No. of electrons = 5

2, 3

Aluminium, Al
Atomic No. = 13
No. of electrons = 13

2, 8, 3

GROUP 4

Carbon, C
Atomic No. = 6
No. of electrons = 6

2, 4

Silicon, Si
Atomic No. = 14
No. of electrons = 14

2, 8, 4

GROUP 5

Nitrogen, N
Atomic No. = 7
No. of electrons = 7

2, 5

Phosphorus, P
Atomic No. = 15
No. of electrons = 15

2, 8, 5

GROUP 6

Oxygen, O
Atomic No. = 8
No. of electrons = 8

2, 6

Sulfur, S
Atomic No. = 16
No. of electrons = 16

2, 8, 6

GROUP 7

Fluorine, F
Atomic No. = 9
No. of electrons = 9

2, 7

Chlorine, Cl
Atomic No. = 17
No. of electrons = 17

2, 8, 7

GROUP 8

Helium, He
Atomic No. = 2
No. of electrons = 2

2

Neon, Ne
Atomic No. = 10
No. of electrons = 10

2, 8

Argon, Ar
Atomic No. = 18
No. of electrons = 18

2, 8, 8

This table is arranged in order of atomic (proton) numbers, placing the elements in groups.

Elements in the same group have the same number of electrons in their highest occupied energy level (outer shell).

Electron configuration of oxygen is 2, 6 because there are...
- 2 electrons in this shell
- 6 electrons in this shell.

How Atoms Combine – Ionic Bonding

Ions, Atoms and Molecules

An **uncharged** particle is either…
- an atom on its own, e.g. Na, Cl
- a molecule of two or more atoms bonded together, e.g. Cl_2, CO_2.

An ion is a charged atom or group of atoms, e.g. Na^+, Cl^-, NH_4^+, SO_4^{2-}.

Forming Ions

A **positive ion** is formed when an atom or group of atoms loses one or more electrons.

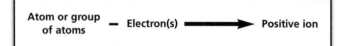

- Losing 1 electron makes a + ion, e.g. Na^+.
- Losing 2 electrons makes a 2+ ion, e.g. Mg^{2+}.
- Losing 3 electrons makes a 3+ ion, e.g. Al^{3+}.

A **negative ion** is formed when an atom or group of atoms gains one or more electrons.

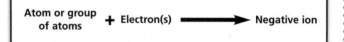

- Gaining 1 electron makes a – ion, e.g. Cl^-.
- Gaining 2 electrons makes a 2– ion, e.g. O^{2-}.

Ionic Bonding

A **metal** and a **non-metal** combine by **transferring electrons**. The metal atoms transfer electrons to become positive ions and the non-metal atoms receive electrons to become negative ions.

The positive ions and negative ions are then **attracted** to each other. Two compounds that are **bonded** through the attraction of oppositely charged ions are sodium chloride and magnesium oxide.

Sodium chloride has a high melting point. It does not conduct electricity when it is solid. However, it can dissolve in water, and the solution produced can conduct electricity. It is also able to conduct electricity when it is molten.

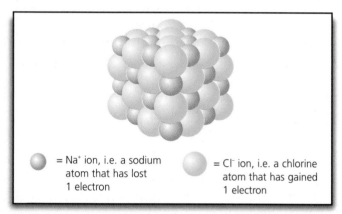

= Na^+ ion, i.e. a sodium atom that has lost 1 electron

= Cl^- ion, i.e. a chlorine atom that has gained 1 electron

Magnesium oxide also has a high melting point. It does not conduct electricity when it is solid. However, it can conduct electricity when it is molten.

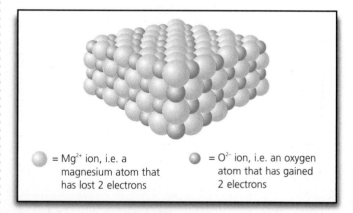

= Mg^{2+} ion, i.e. a magnesium atom that has lost 2 electrons

= O^{2-} ion, i.e. an oxygen atom that has gained 2 electrons

Structure and Physical Properties of NaCl and MgO

Sodium chloride (NaCl) and magnesium oxide (MgO) form **giant ionic lattices** in which positive ions and negative ions are **electrostatically** attracted to each other. This attraction between oppositely charged ions results in them having high melting points. They conduct electricity when molten or in solution because the charged ions are free to move about. When they are solid, the ions are held in place and cannot move about, which means they do not conduct electricity.

How Atoms Combine – Ionic Bonding

29

The Ionic Bond

When a **metal** and a **non-metal** combine, electrons are transferred from one atom to the other to form **ions**, each of which has a **complete outer shell** (a stable octet).

Example 1

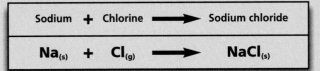

Sodium	+	Chlorine	→	Sodium chloride
$Na_{(s)}$	+	$Cl_{(g)}$	→	$NaCl_{(s)}$

The sodium atom has 1 electron in its outer shell which is transferred to the chlorine atom to give them both 8 electrons in their outer shell. The atoms become ions (Na^+ and Cl^-) and the compound formed is sodium chloride, NaCl.

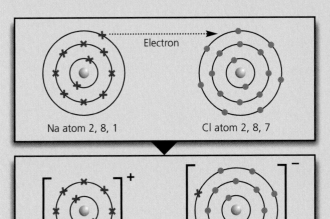

Na atom 2, 8, 1   Cl atom 2, 8, 7

Na^+ ion $[2, 8]^+$ Cl^- ion $[2, 8, 8]^-$

Example 2

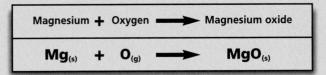

Magnesium	+	Oxygen	→	Magnesium oxide
$Mg_{(s)}$	+	$O_{(g)}$	→	$MgO_{(s)}$

The magnesium atom has 2 electrons in its outer shell which are transferred to the oxygen atom to give them both 8 electrons in their outer shell. The atoms become ions (Mg^{2+} and O^{2-}) and the compound formed is magnesium oxide, MgO.

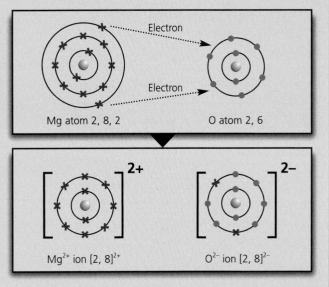

Electron

Electron

Mg atom 2, 8, 2   O atom 2, 6

Mg^{2+} ion $[2, 8]^{2+}$ O^{2-} ion $[2, 8]^{2-}$

Example 3

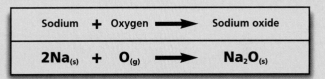

Sodium	+	Oxygen	→	Sodium oxide
$2Na_{(s)}$	+	$O_{(g)}$	→	$Na_2O_{(s)}$

The sodium atom has 1 electron in its outer shell. An oxygen atom needs 2 electrons, therefore, 2 Na atoms are needed. The atoms become ions (Na^+, Na^+ and O^{2-}) and the compound formed is sodium oxide, Na_2O.

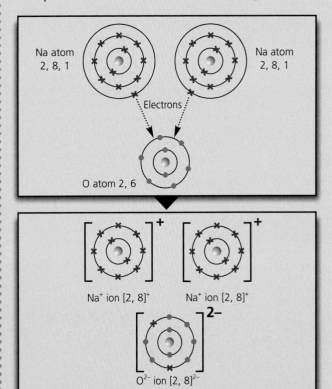

Na atom 2, 8, 1   Na atom 2, 8, 1

Electrons

O atom 2, 6

Na^+ ion $[2, 8]^+$ Na^+ ion $[2, 8]^+$

O^{2-} ion $[2, 8]^{2-}$

The Ionic Bond (cont.)

Example 4

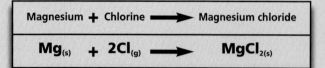

Magnesium + Chlorine → Magnesium chloride

$$Mg_{(s)} + 2Cl_{(g)} \longrightarrow MgCl_{2(s)}$$

The magnesium atom has 2 electrons in its outer shell. A chlorine atom only needs 1 electron, therefore, 2 Cl atoms are needed. The atoms become ions (Mg^{2+}, Cl^- and Cl^-) and the compound formed is magnesium chloride, $MgCl_2$ (see diagram below).

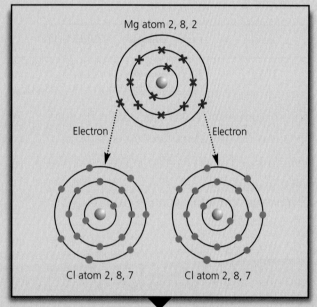

Mg atom 2, 8, 2

Electron   Electron

Cl atom 2, 8, 7   Cl atom 2, 8, 7

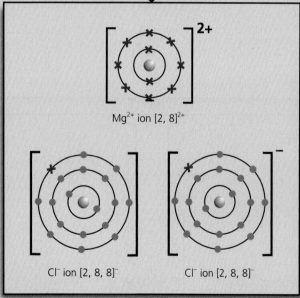

Mg^{2+} ion $[2, 8]^{2+}$

Cl^- ion $[2, 8, 8]^-$ Cl^- ion $[2, 8, 8]^-$

Formulae of Ionic Compounds

All ionic compounds are neutral substances that have equal charges on the positive ion(s) and negative ion(s). The table below shows how ions with different charges combine to form ionic compounds.

Positive Ions	Negative Ions	
	1– e.g. Cl^-, OH^-	**2–** e.g. SO_4^{2-}, O^{2-}
1+ e.g. K^+, Na^+	KCl — 1+ ↘ 1–	K_2SO_4 — 2 x 1+ = 2+ ↘ 2–
	$NaOH$ — 1+ ↘ 1–	Na_2O — 2 x 1+ = 2+ ↘ 2–
2+ e.g. Mg^{2+}, Cu^{2+}	$MgCl_2$ — 2+ ↘ 2 x 1– = 2–	$MgSO_4$ — 2+ ↘ 2–
	$Cu(OH)_2$ — 2+ ↘ 2 x 1– = 2–	CuO — 2+ ↘ 2–
3+ e.g. Al^{3+}, Fe^{3+}	$AlCl_3$ — 3+ ↘ 3 x 1– = 3–	$Al_2(SO_4)_3$ — 2 x 3+ = 6+ ↘ 3 x 2– = 6–
	$Fe(OH)_3$ — 3+ ↘ 3 x 1– = 3–	Fe_2O_3 — 2 x 3+ = 6+ ↘ 3 x 2– = 6–

Covalent Bonding & The Periodic Table

The Periodic Table

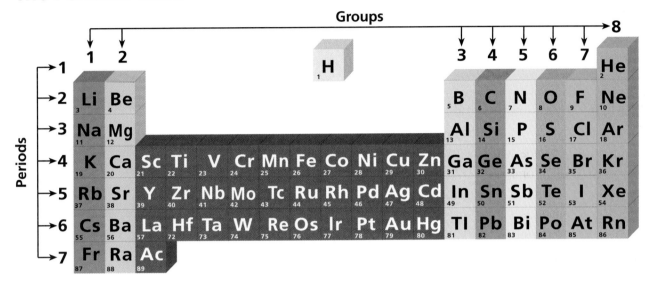

Elements are the building blocks of all materials. The 100 or so elements are arranged in order of **ascending atomic number**, and then arranged in rows (periods) so that elements with similar properties are in the same column (group). This forms the basis of the **periodic table**. More than three-quarters of the elements are metals. The others are non-metals.

Groups

A vertical column of elements in the periodic table is called a group, e.g. Group 1 contains lithium (Li), sodium (Na) and potassium (K), among others. Elements in the same group have similar chemical properties. This is because they have the **same** number of electrons in their outer shell. This number also coincides with the group number, e.g.

- Group 1 elements have 1 electron in their outer shell
- Group 7 elements have 7 electrons in their outer shell
- Group 8 elements have 8 electrons in their outer shell.

Periods

A **horizontal row** of elements in the periodic table is called a **period**, e.g. lithium (Li), carbon (C) and neon (Ne) are all elements in the second period.

The period to which the element belongs corresponds to the **number of shells of electrons** it has, e.g. sodium (Na), aluminium (Al) and chlorine (Cl) all have three shells of electrons so they are found in the third period.

Bonding

A molecule is two or more atoms bonded together. There are two types of bonding:

- **covalent** bonding – non-metals combine by sharing electrons
- **ionic** bonding – metals and non-metals combine by transferring electrons (see p.28 – 30).

Two examples of covalently bonded molecules are **water** and **carbon dioxide**.

Water, H_2O…

- is a liquid with a low melting point
- does not conduct electricity.

A molecule of water is made up of 1 atom of oxygen and 2 atoms of hydrogen.

Carbon dioxide, CO_2…

- is a gas with a low melting point
- does not conduct electricity.

A molecule of carbon dioxide is made up of 1 atom of carbon and 2 atoms of oxygen.

Covalent Bonding & The Periodic Table

Representing Atoms

The following are all examples of covalently bonded molecules. You need to be familiar with how they are formed:

Water (H₂O) – the outer shells of the hydrogen and oxygen atoms overlap and the oxygen atom shares a pair of electrons with each hydrogen atom to form a water molecule.

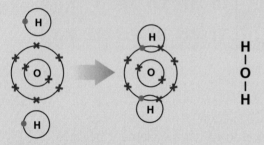

Hydrogen (H₂) – the two hydrogen atoms share a pair of electrons.

Methane (CH₄) – the carbon atom shares a pair of electrons with each hydrogen atom.

Chlorine (Cl₂) – the two chlorine atoms share a pair of electrons.

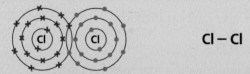

Carbon dioxide (CO₂) – the outer shells of the carbon and oxygen atoms overlap and the carbon atom shares two pairs of electrons with each oxygen atom to form a double covalently bonded molecule.

Properties of Simple Covalently Bonded Molecules

The bond between two atoms in a simple covalently bonded molecule (e.g. water or carbon dioxide) is very strong. The **intermolecular forces** of attraction between molecules are weak. This results in them having low melting points. They do not conduct electricity as they do not have any free electrons.

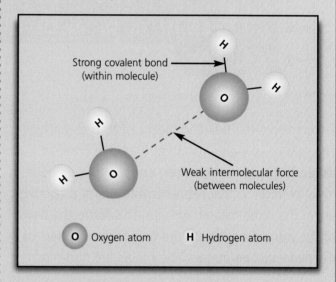

Refer back to electronic configuration on p.26. You have already learnt that there is a connection between...
- the number of electrons in an element's outer shell and the group it can be found in
- the number of shells of electrons an element has and the period it can be found in.

So, if you are given an element's electronic structure, you can deduce its position in the periodic table. For example, sulfur's electronic structure is 2,8,6. This tells us it has 3 electron shells, which means it can be found in the third period, and it has 6 electrons in its outer shell, so it can be found in Group 6.

By looking at the periodic table, you can deduce an element's electronic structure. For example, aluminium is in Group 3 in the third period, so its electronic structure is 2,8,3.

Group 1 – The Alkali Metals

The **alkali metals** occupy the first vertical column (**Group 1**) at the left-hand side of the periodic table. The first three elements in the group are lithium, sodium and potassium. They all have one electron in their outer shell which means they have similar properties. Alkali metals are stored under oil because they react with air and react vigorously with water.

Flame Tests

Lithium, sodium and potassium compounds can be recognised by the colours they produce in a **flame test**. The method used is explained below:

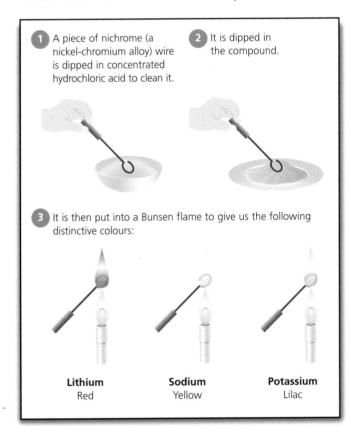

1 A piece of nichrome (a nickel-chromium alloy) wire is dipped in concentrated hydrochloric acid to clean it.

2 It is dipped in the compound.

3 It is then put into a Bunsen flame to give us the following distinctive colours:

| **Lithium** | **Sodium** | **Potassium** |
| Red | Yellow | Lilac |

Reacting Alkali Metals with Water

Alkali metals react with water to produce hydrogen and a **hydroxide.** Alkali metal hydroxides are soluble and form **alkaline solutions**.

As we go **down** the group, the alkali metals become more reactive and so they react more vigorously with water. They all float and some may melt and produce hydrogen gas (which may ignite).

Lithium reacts gently, sodium reacts more aggressively and potassium reacts so aggressively that it melts and burns with a lilac flame.

The diagram below shows clearly what happens when a small piece of potassium is dropped into water:

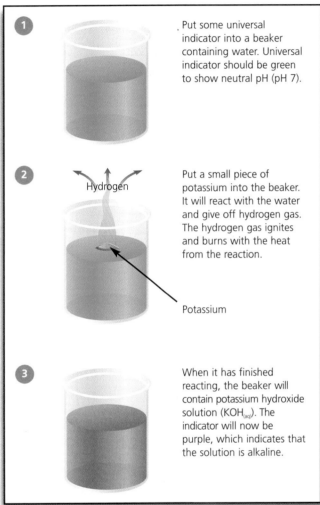

1 Put some universal indicator into a beaker containing water. Universal indicator should be green to show neutral pH (pH 7).

2 Put a small piece of potassium into the beaker. It will react with the water and give off hydrogen gas. The hydrogen gas ignites and burns with the heat from the reaction.

Hydrogen

Potassium

3 When it has finished reacting, the beaker will contain potassium hydroxide solution ($KOH_{(aq)}$). The indicator will now be purple, which indicates that the solution is alkaline.

| Lithium | + | Water | ⟶ | Lithium hydroxide | + | Hydrogen |

HT $2Li_{(s)} + 2H_2O_{(l)} \longrightarrow 2LiOH_{(aq)} + H_{2(g)}$

| Sodium | + | Water | ⟶ | Sodium hydroxide | + | Hydrogen |

HT $2Na_{(s)} + 2H_2O_{(l)} \longrightarrow 2NaOH_{(aq)} + H_{2(g)}$

| Potassium | + | Water | ⟶ | Potassium hydroxide | + | Hydrogen |

HT $2K_{(s)} + 2H_2O_{(l)} \longrightarrow 2KOH_{(aq)} + H_{2(g)}$

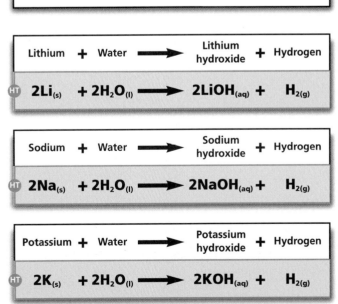

The Group 1 Elements

More on the Alkali Metals

Even though the alkali metals have similar chemical properties, their physical properties alter as we go down the group.

The table below contains their melting and boiling points and their densities:

Element	Melting Point (°C)	Boiling Point (°C)	Density (g/cm³)
Lithium, Li	180	1340	0.53
Sodium, Na	98	883	0.97
Potassium, K	64	760	0.86
Rubidium, Rb	39	688	1.53
Caesium, Cs	29	671	1.90

The melting points and boiling points of alkali metals decrease as we go down the group.

Rubidium is the fourth element in Group 1. Rubidium, like the other elements in the group, would react with water. The reaction would be...

• very fast
• exothermic
• violent (if it is carried out in a glass beaker, the beaker may shatter).

Caesium (the fifth element in the group) has the lowest melting and boiling points.

Generally, the density increases as we go down the group (except for potassium). Caesium has the greatest density.

Trends in Group 1

Alkali metals have similar properties because, when they react, an atom loses one electron to form a **positive ion** with a **stable electronic structure**, i.e. it has a full outer shell of electrons.

The alkali metals become more reactive as we go down the group because the outer shell gets further away from the influence of the nucleus, making it easier for an atom to lose an electron from this shell.

Oxidation involves the loss of electrons by an atom, for example...

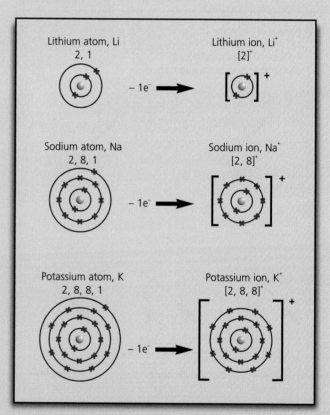

Lithium atom, Li 2, 1 — $-1e^-$ → Lithium ion, Li^+ $[2]^+$

Sodium atom, Na 2, 8, 1 — $-1e^-$ → Sodium ion, Na^+ $[2, 8]^+$

Potassium atom, K 2, 8, 8, 1 — $-1e^-$ → Potassium ion, K^+ $[2, 8, 8]^+$

The equations for the formation of the Group 1 metal ions are usually written as follows...

$$Li_{(s)} \longrightarrow Li^+_{(s)} + e^-$$

$$Na_{(s)} \longrightarrow Na^+_{(s)} + e^-$$

$$K_{(s)} \longrightarrow K^+_{(s)} + e^-$$

Group 7 – The Halogens

There are five non-metals in Group 7 and they are known as the **halogens**. They all have seven electrons in their outer shell which means that they have similar chemical properties. You need to know about four of the halogens: **fluorine**, **chlorine**, **bromine** and **iodine**.

At room temperature…
- fluorine is a pale yellow gas
- chlorine is a green gas
- bromine is an orange liquid
- iodine is a grey solid.

Iodine is used as an antiseptic to sterilise wounds.

Chlorine, the most commonly used halogen, is used to sterilise water and to make pesticides and plastics. It is extracted from sodium chloride (common salt) by electrolysis.

As well as being used to produce chlorine, sodium chloride can also be used as…
- a flavouring
- a preservative.

Reactions with Alkali Metals

Halogens react vigorously with alkali metals to form metal halides, e.g.

Lithium + Chlorine ⟶ Lithium chloride

HT $2Li_{(s)} + Cl_{2(g)} \longrightarrow 2LiCl_{(s)}$

Displacement Reactions

As we go down the group, the halogens become **less reactive**, and their melting and boiling points increase.

Fluorine is therefore the most reactive halogen and iodine is the least reactive.

A more reactive halogen will displace a less reactive halogen from an aqueous solution of its metal halide, i.e. chlorine will displace bromides and iodides, and bromine will displace iodides.

If we were to pass chlorine gas through an aqueous solution of potassium bromide, bromine would be formed due to the displacement reaction taking place:

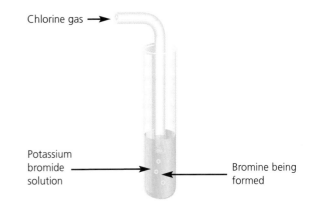

Chlorine gas

Potassium bromide solution

Bromine being formed

The table below shows the results of reactions between halogens and aqueous solutions of salts:

	Potassium Chloride	Potassium Bromide	Potassium Iodide
Chlorine Cl_2	✕	Potassium chloride	Potassium chloride
Bromine Br_2	No reaction	✕	Potassium bromide
Iodine I_2	No reaction	No reaction	✕

✕ = No experiment conducted.

Potassium bromide + Chlorine ⟶ Potassium chloride + Bromine

HT $2KBr_{(aq)} + Cl_{2(g)} \longrightarrow 2KCl_{(aq)} + Br_{2(aq)}$

Potassium iodide + Chlorine ⟶ Potassium chloride + Iodine

HT $2KI_{(aq)} + Cl_{2(g)} \longrightarrow 2KCl_{(aq)} + I_{2(aq)}$

Potassium iodide + Bromine ⟶ Potassium bromide + Iodine

HT $2KI_{(aq)} + Br_{2(l)} \longrightarrow 2KBr_{(aq)} + I_{2(aq)}$

The Group 7 Elements

More on the Halogens

Fluorine is the first element in Group 7, and is the most reactive element in the group. It will displace all of the other halogens from an aqueous solution of their metal halides.

Astatine is the fifth element in Group 7. It is a semi-metallic, radioactive element and only very small amounts of it exist naturally. Even so, it is the least reactive of the halogens and, theoretically, it would be unable to displace any of the other halogens from an aqueous solution of their metal halides.

The **physical properties** of the halogens alter as we go down the group. The table below contains their melting and boiling points and their densities:

Element	Melting Point (°C)	Boiling Point (°C)	Density (g/cm³)
Fluorine, F	-220	-188	0.0016
Chlorine, Cl	-101	-34	0.003
Bromine, Br	-7	59	3.12
Iodine, I	114	184	4.95
Astatine, At	302 (estimated)	337 (estimated)	Not known

The melting points and boiling points of the halogens increase as we go down the group. Astatine is estimated to have the highest melting and boiling points.

The density increases as we go down the group. However, astatine's density is not known as it has a very **unstable nature**.

Trends in Group 7

The halogens have similar properties because, when they react, an atom **gains** one electron to form a **negative ion** with a stable electronic structure, i.e. it has a full outer shell of electrons. **Reduction** involves the gain of electrons by an atom, for example...

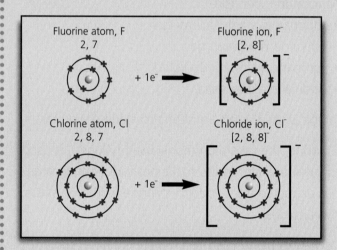

Fluorine atom, F 2, 7   + 1e⁻   Fluorine ion, F⁻ [2, 8]⁻

Chlorine atom, Cl 2, 8, 7   + 1e⁻   Chloride ion, Cl⁻ [2, 8, 8]⁻

The halogens become less reactive as we go down the group because the outer shell gets further away from the influence of the nucleus, making it harder for an atom to gain an electron.

The equations for the formation of the halide ions from halogen molecules are usually written as follows:

$$F_{2(s)} + 2e^- \longrightarrow 2F^-_{(s)}$$

$$Cl_{2(g)} + 2e^- \longrightarrow 2Cl^-_{(g)}$$

You can decide whether a reaction is an example of oxidation or reduction by looking at its equation, such as the ones above. If electrons are added, then it is a reduction reaction, and if electrons are taken away it is an oxidation reaction.

An easy way to remember the definitions of oxidation and reduction is **OILRIG**:
Oxidation **I**s **L**oss of electrons
Reduction **I**s **G**ain of electrons.

Electrolysis

Some compounds **conduct electricity** when they are
molten (melted) or in **solution**, but not otherwise.
In these cases, the liquid or solution must contain
ions. A liquid or solution that conducts electricity
is called an **electrolyte**. An electrolyte can be
separated into its constituent parts by electrolysis.

When a direct current is passed through an electrolyte,
the compound will **decompose** (break down) and
elements will be produced. This is because the ions
move to the electrode of opposite charge:

- The ions that are positively charged move
  towards the negative electrode (the cathode);
  they are called **cations**.
- The ions that are negatively charged move
  towards the positive electrode (the anode); they
  are called **anions**.

When they get there, they lose their charges: they
are **discharged**. The negative ions lose electrons to
the anode, and the positive ions gain electrons from
the cathode, to form atoms of elements.

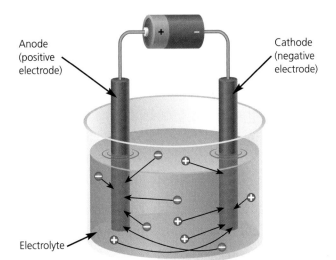

Electrolysis of Sulfuric Acid

Sulfuric acid is an electrolyte. It contains hydrogen
ions (H^+ cations) and hydroxide ions (OH^- anions).

When dilute sulfuric acid undergoes electrolysis (see
diagram below)…
- the hydrogen cations are attracted to the
  cathode and form hydrogen gas
- the hydroxide anions are attracted to the anode
  and form oxygen gas.

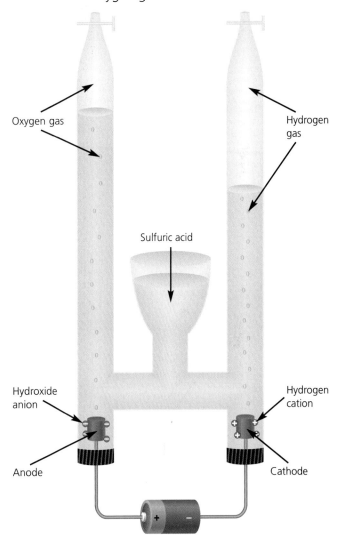

The reactions at the electrodes can be written
as half-equations. This means that separate
equations are written to show what is happening
at each of the electrodes during electrolysis.

The electrolysis of dilute sulfuric acid can be
represented by the following two **half-equations**:

- at the cathode:

$$2H^+_{(aq)} + 2e^- \xrightarrow{Reduction} H_{2(g)}$$

- at the anode:

$$4OH^-_{(aq)} - 4e^- \xrightarrow{Oxidation} 2H_2O_{(l)} + O_{2(g)}$$

Electrolysis

Electrolysis of Sulfuric Acid (cont.)

The products of the electrolysis of sulfuric acid can be **tested** as follows:

- hydrogen burns with a squeaky pop when tested with a lighted splint

Hydrogen

Lighted splint

Pop!

- oxygen re-lights a glowing splint.

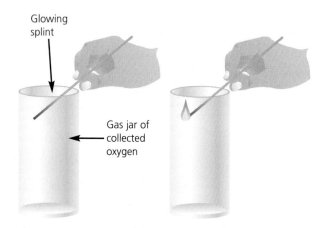

Glowing splint

Gas jar of collected oxygen

Extracting Aluminium

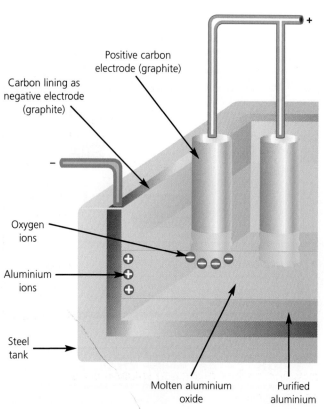

Positive carbon electrode (graphite)

Carbon lining as negative electrode (graphite)

Oxygen ions

Aluminium ions

Steel tank

Molten aluminium oxide

Purified aluminium

Aluminium must be obtained from its ore by electrolysis because it is too reactive to be extracted by heating with carbon. The electrodes are made of graphite (a type of carbon). The aluminium ore (bauxite) is purified to leave aluminium oxide, which is then melted so that the ions can move.

When a current passes through the molten mixture…

- positively charged aluminium ions move towards the negative electrode (the cathode) and form aluminium
- negatively charged oxygen ions move towards the positive electrodes (the anodes) and form oxygen.

The positive electrodes gradually wear away, which means they have to be replaced every so often. Extracting aluminium can be quite an expensive process because of the cost of the large amounts of electrical energy needed to carry it out.

The electrolysis of aluminium can be represented by the following equation:

Aluminium oxide $\longrightarrow$ Aluminium $+$ Oxygen

HT $$2Al_2O_{3(l)} \longrightarrow 4Al_{(l)} + 3O_{2(g)}$$

HT In the extraction of aluminium, the aluminium oxide is mixed with cryolite (a compound of aluminium) to lower its melting point. This reduces the energy needed for the process.

The electrolysis of molten aluminium oxide can be represented by the following two half-equations:

- at the cathode:

$$Al^{3+}_{(l)} + 3e^- \xrightarrow{\text{Reduction}} Al_{(l)}$$

- at the anode:

$$2O^{2-}_{(l)} \xrightarrow{\text{Oxidation}} O_{2(g)} + 4e^-$$

The Transition Metals

In the centre of the periodic table, between Groups 2 and 3, is a block of metallic elements called the **transition metals**. This block includes **iron** (Fe), **copper** (Cu), **platinum** (Pt), **mercury** (Hg), **chromium** (Cr), and **zinc** (Zn).

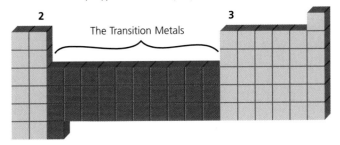

Transition metals have the typical properties of metals (see p.40).

Compounds of transition metals are often **coloured**:
*   copper compounds are blue
*   iron (II) compounds are grey–green
*   iron (III) compounds are orange–brown.

Many transition metals and their compounds can be used as **catalysts** in chemical reactions, for example...
*   iron is used in the Haber process
*   nickel is used in the manufacture of margarine.

Thermal Decomposition of Transition Metal Carbonates

Thermal decomposition is a reaction where a substance is broken down into simpler substances by heating. When transition metal carbonates are heated, a **colour change** occurs and they decompose to form a **metal oxide** and **carbon dioxide**. For example, if copper carbonate is heated, the blue–green copper carbonate decomposes into black copper oxide and carbon dioxide, which turns limewater milky (see diagram below).

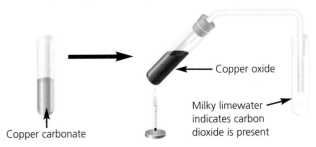

Copper carbonate

Copper oxide

Milky limewater indicates carbon dioxide is present

| Copper (II) carbonate | → | Copper (II) oxide | + | Carbon dioxide |

HT $CuCO_{3(s)} \longrightarrow CuO_{(s)} + CO_{2(g)}$

| Iron (II) carbonate | → | Iron (II) oxide | + | Carbon dioxide |

HT $FeCO_{3(s)} \longrightarrow FeO_{(s)} + CO_{2(g)}$

| Manganese carbonate | → | Manganese oxide | + | Carbon dioxide |

HT $MnCO_{3(s)} \longrightarrow MnO_{(s)} + CO_{2(g)}$

| Zinc carbonate | → | Zinc oxide | + | Carbon dioxide |

HT $ZnCO_{3(s)} \longrightarrow ZnO_{(s)} + CO_{2(g)}$

Identifying Transition Metal Ions

Metal compounds in solution contain metal ions. Some of these form **precipitates** (insoluble solids) that come out of solution when sodium hydroxide solution is added to them. The following ions form coloured precipitates:

Metal Ion	Colour of Precipitate	Ionic Symbol Equation
Copper (II), Cu^{2+}	Blue	**HT** $Cu^{2+}_{(aq)} + 2OH^-_{(aq)} \longrightarrow Cu(OH)_{2(s)}$
Iron (II), Fe^{2+}	Grey–green **HT**	$Fe^{2+}_{(aq)} + 2OH^-_{(aq)} \longrightarrow Fe(OH)_{2(s)}$
Iron (III), Fe^{3+}	Orange–brown **HT**	$Fe^{3+}_{(aq)} + 3OH^-_{(aq)} \longrightarrow Fe(OH)_{3(s)}$

N.B. The reaction between the transition metal ions and sodium hydroxide solution is known as precipitation.

Metal Structure and Properties

Iron and Copper

Iron and copper are two transition metals that have many uses, for example…

- iron is used to make steel, which is used to make cars and girders because it is **very strong**
- copper is used to make electrical wiring because it is a **good conductor**.

Physical Properties

Metals are very useful materials because of their properties. They…

- are **lustrous** (shiny), e.g. gold is used in jewellery
- are **hard** and have a **high density**, e.g. steel is used to make drill bits
- have high **tensile strength** (able to bear loads), e.g. steel is used to make girders
- have **high melting** and **boiling points**, e.g. tungsten is used to make light bulb filaments
- are **good conductors** of heat and electricity, e.g. copper is used to make saucepans and wiring.

Metal Structure

Metal atoms are packed very close together in a regular arrangement (see diagram below). The atoms are held together by metallic bonds.

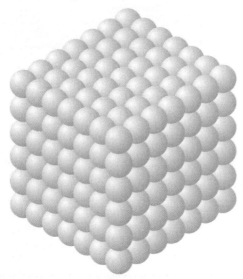

Metals have high melting and boiling points because lots of energy is needed to overcome the strong metallic bonds. As the metal atoms pack together, they build a structure of **crystals**.

Superconductors

Metals are able to conduct electricity because the atoms are very close together and the electrons can move from atom to atom.

At low temperatures, some metals can become **superconductors**. A superconductor has very little, or no, resistance to the flow of electricity. Very low resistance is useful when you require…

- a powerful electromagnet, e.g. inside medical scanners
- very fast electronic circuits, e.g. in a supercomputer
- power transmission that does not lose energy.

Metallic Structure

Metal atoms are packed so close together that the outer electron shells **overlap** and form **metallic bonds**. The overlap allows electrons to move about freely. The structure can be described as closely packed metal ions in a 'sea' of **delocalised** (free) electrons.

Delocalised electron → ← Metal ion

The free movement of the delocalised electrons allows the metal to conduct electricity (e.g. in wiring). The metal is held together by strong forces (the **electrostatic attraction** between the metal ions and the delocalised electrons). This is why the metal structure has high melting and boiling points.

More About Superconductors

The search is on to find a superconductor that will work at room temperature (20°C). The majority of superconductors currently in use operate at temperatures below -200°C. This very low temperature is costly to maintain and impractical for large-scale uses.

Measuring Speed

One way to describe the movement of an object is by measuring its **speed**, i.e. how fast it is moving. Speed is measured in **metres per second (m/s)**, **kilometres per hour (km/h)** or **miles per hour (mph)**. Since the cyclist in the diagram above travels a distance of 8 metres every second, we can say that the speed of the cyclist is 8m/s.

If we want to work out the speed of any moving object we need to know two things:

- the **distance** it travels (which can be measured using a measuring tape or a trundle wheel)
- the **time taken** to travel that distance (which can be measured using a stopwatch or stopclock).

We can then calculate the speed of the object using the following equation:

$$\text{Speed (m/s)} = \frac{\text{Distance travelled (m)}}{\text{Time taken (s)}}$$

where v is speed

$$\frac{d}{v \times t}$$

- The faster the speed of an object, the greater the distance it travels in a particular time.
- The faster the speed of an object, the shorter the time it takes to travel a particular distance.

Example 1

Calculate the speed of a cyclist who travels 2400m in 5 minutes.

Use the formula…

$$\text{Speed} = \frac{\text{Distance}}{\text{Time taken}}$$
$$= \frac{2400\text{m}}{300\text{s}} = \textbf{8m/s}$$

Time must be in seconds if distance is in metres

HT You need to be able to rearrange the speed formula in order to calculate either distance or time taken.

Example 2

A car is travelling at a constant speed of 80km/h. Calculate the distance it travels in 90 minutes.

Rearrange the formula…

Distance = Speed x Time taken
$$= 80\text{km/h} \times 1.5\text{h}$$
$$= \textbf{120km}$$

Time must be in hours if speed is in kilometres per hour

Example 3

Calculate the time it takes a motorcyclist to travel a distance of 120km at 50km/h.

Rearrange the formula…

$$\text{Time taken} = \frac{\text{Distance}}{\text{Speed}}$$
$$= \frac{120\text{km}}{50\text{km/h}}$$
$$= 2.4\text{h} = \textbf{2h 24min}$$

You need to convert the decimal into minutes

Speed cameras generally take two pictures of a vehicle, one a certain amount of time after the other.

The position of the vehicle in relation to the distance markings on the road in the two pictures can be used to calculate the speed of the vehicle, using this formula…

$$\text{Speed of car} = \frac{\text{Distance travelled between pictures}}{\text{Time between first and second picture}}$$

Speed

Distance–Time Graphs

The slope of a **distance–time graph** represents the speed of an object; the steeper the slope, the greater the speed.

The y-axis shows the distance from a fixed point (0), not total distance travelled.

If an object (e.g. a person) is standing 10m from point (0) and not moving, the distance–time graph would look like this:

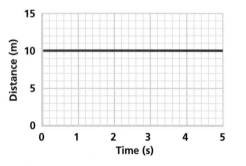 

$$\frac{10 - 10}{5} = 0\text{m/s}$$

If the person starts at point (0) and moves at a constant speed of 2m/s, the graph would look like this:

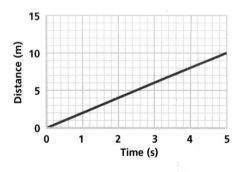 

$$\frac{10 - 0}{5} = 2\text{m/s}$$

If the person starts at point (0) and moves at a greater constant speed of 3m/s, the graph would look like this:

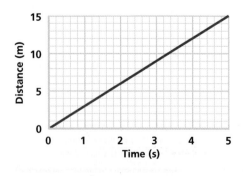 

$$\frac{15 - 0}{5} = 3\text{m/s}$$

HT The speed of an object can be calculated by working out the **gradient** of a **distance–time graph**: the steeper the gradient, the faster the speed. Take any point on the graph and read off the distance travelled for that part of the journey and the time taken to get there.

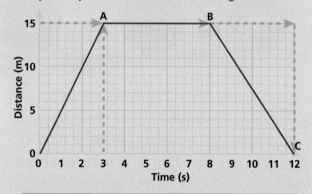

0 to A: Substitute figures into the formula:

$$v = \frac{d}{t} = \frac{15 - 0\text{m}}{3\text{s}} = \textbf{5m/s}$$

A to B: Object stationary (no slope). Prove this using the formula:

$$v = \frac{d}{t} = \frac{15 - 15\text{m}}{5\text{s}} = \textbf{0m/s}$$

B to C: Substitute figures into the formula:

$$v = \frac{d}{t} = \frac{15 - 0\text{m}}{4\text{s}} = \textbf{3.75m/s}$$

So, the object travelled at 5m/s for 3 seconds, remained stationary for 5 seconds then travelled at 3.75m/s for 4 seconds back to the starting point.

Distance–Time Graphs for Non-Uniform Speed

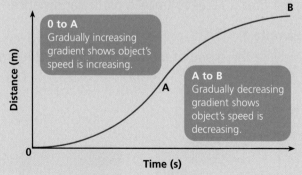

0 to A Gradually increasing gradient shows object's speed is increasing.

A to B Gradually decreasing gradient shows object's speed is decreasing.

Measuring Acceleration

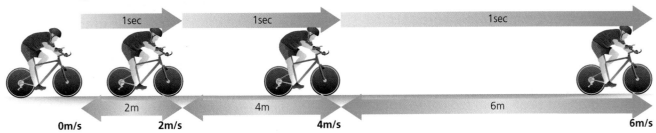

The **acceleration** of an object is the **change in speed per second**. In other words, it is a measure of how quickly an object speeds up or slows down. **Acceleration** has only one unit: **metres per second per second (m/s²)**. Since the cyclist in the illustration above increases his speed by 2 metres per second every second, we can say that his acceleration is 2m/s² (2 metres per second, per second).

If we want to work out the acceleration of any moving object we need to know two things:

- the change in speed
- the time taken for this change in speed.

The acceleration or deceleration of the object can then be calculated using the following formula:

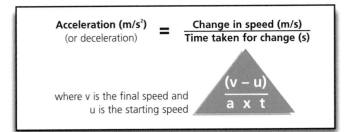

There are two points to be aware of:

- the cyclist in the diagram above increases his speed by the **same amount** every second which means the **distance** he travels each second increases
- deceleration is simply a negative acceleration, i.e. it describes an object that is slowing down.

Example 1

A cyclist accelerates uniformly from rest and reaches a speed of 10m/s after 5 seconds. He then decelerates uniformly and comes to rest in a further 10 seconds.

a) Calculate his acceleration.

Use the formula…

$$a = \frac{(v - u)}{t} = \frac{10 - 0\text{m/s}}{5\text{s}} = \textbf{2m/s}^2$$

b) Calculate his deceleration.

Again, use the formula…

$$a = \frac{(v - u)}{t} = \frac{0 - 10\text{m/s}}{10\text{s}} = \textbf{-1m/s}^2$$

> i.e. a deceleration of 1m/s²

Example 2

An object at rest falls from the top of a building with an acceleration of 10m/s². It hits the ground with a speed of 25m/s. Calculate how long the object takes to fall.

Rearrange the formula…

$$\text{Time taken} = \frac{\text{Change in speed}}{\text{Acceleration}}$$

$$= \frac{25\text{m/s} - 0}{10\text{m/s}^2} = \textbf{2.5s}$$

Example 3

A car accelerates at 1.5m/s² for 12 seconds. If the initial speed of the car was 10m/s, calculate the speed of the car after the acceleration.

Rearrange the formula…

Change in speed = Acceleration x Time taken

$$= 1.5\text{m/s}^2 \times 12\text{s}$$

$$= \textbf{18m/s}$$

$$\frac{\text{Speed of car}}{\text{after acceleration}} = \frac{\text{Initial}}{\text{speed}} + \frac{\text{Change in}}{\text{speed}}$$

$$= 10\text{m/s} + 18\text{m/s}$$

$$= \textbf{28m/s}$$

*N.B. Acceleration can involve a **change of direction** as well as speed.*

Changing Speed

Speed–Time Graphs

The slope of a **speed–time graph** represents the acceleration of the object. A constant acceleration increases the speed. The steeper the slope (from bottom left to top right), the greater the acceleration. A negative gradient slope (from top left to bottom right) indicates deceleration (decreasing speed).

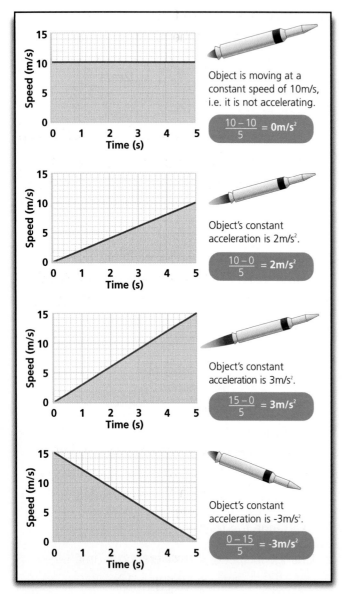

Object is moving at a constant speed of 10m/s, i.e. it is not accelerating.
$$\frac{10-10}{5} = 0m/s^2$$

Object's constant acceleration is 2m/s².
$$\frac{10-0}{5} = 2m/s^2$$

Object's constant acceleration is 3m/s².
$$\frac{15-0}{5} = 3m/s^2$$

Object's constant acceleration is -3m/s².
$$\frac{0-15}{5} = -3m/s^2$$

The area underneath the line in a speed–time graph represents the total distance travelled. For example, the area under the line in the third graph ($\frac{1}{2}$ x 15 x 5 = 37.5) is greater than the area under the line in the second graph ($\frac{1}{2}$ x 10 x 5 = 25). This means that the distance travelled by the object in the third graph is greater than the distance travelled by the object in the second graph for the same time period.

HT The **acceleration** of an object can be calculated by working out the **gradient** of a **speed–time graph**: the steeper the gradient, the greater the acceleration. All we have to do is take any point on the graph and read off the change in speed over the chosen period, and the time taken for this change.

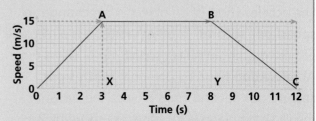

0 to A: Substitute figures into the formula:

$$\text{Acceleration} = \frac{15m/s - 0m/s}{3s} = \textbf{5m/s}^2$$

A to B: Constant speed (no slope = no acceleration). Prove this using the formula:

$$\text{Acceleration} = \frac{15m/s - 15m/s}{5s} = \textbf{0m/s}^2$$

B to C: Substitute figures into the formula:

$$\text{Acceleration} = \frac{0m/s - 15m/s}{4s} = \textbf{-3.75m/s}^2$$

So, the object accelerated at 5m/s² for 3 seconds, then travelled at a constant speed of 15m/s for 5 seconds, and then decelerated at a rate of 3.75m/s² for 4 seconds.

The total distance travelled can be calculated by working out the area under the speed–time graph.

= Area of 0AX + Area of ABYX + Area of BCY
= ($\frac{1}{2}$ x 3 x 15) + (5 x 15) + ($\frac{1}{2}$ x 4 x 15) = **127.5m**

Speed–Time Graph for Non-Uniform Motion

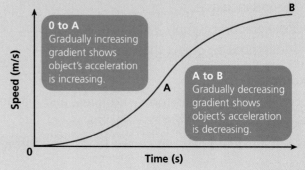

0 to A
Gradually increasing gradient shows object's acceleration is increasing.

A to B
Gradually decreasing gradient shows object's acceleration is decreasing.

Forces and Motion

Forces in Action

Forces are **pushes** or **pulls**. They are measured in **newtons (N)** and may be different in size and act in different directions. Forces can cause objects to speed up or slow down, for example…

- **weight** causes an apple falling from a tree to speed up as it falls
- **friction** causes a car to slow down
- **air resistance** causes a parachutist to slow down after opening the parachute.

Force, Mass and Acceleration

If an unbalanced force acts on an object then the acceleration of the object will depend on…

- the **size** of the unbalanced force – the bigger the force, the greater the acceleration
- the **mass** of the object – the bigger the mass, the smaller the acceleration.

If a boy pushes a trolley, he exerts an unbalanced force which causes the trolley to move and accelerate.

1 second

If two boys push the same trolley, it moves with a greater acceleration. (More force = more acceleration.)

1 second

If one boy pushes a trolley of bigger mass, it moves with a smaller acceleration than the first trolley. (More mass = less acceleration.)

1 second

If two trolleys with different masses move with a constant acceleration, the trolley with the larger mass (see ❶) will have more force than the trolley with the smaller mass (see ❷).

The relationship between force, mass and acceleration is shown in the following formula:

$$\text{Force (N)} = \text{Mass (kg)} \times \text{Acceleration (m/s}^2)$$

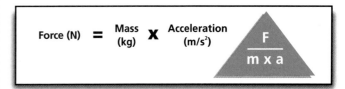

From this formula, we can define a newton (N) as the force needed to give a mass of one kilogram an acceleration of one metre per second per second (1m/s^2).

Example

A trolley of mass 400kg is accelerating at 0.5m/s^2. What force is needed to achieve this acceleration?

Use the formula…

Force = Mass x Acceleration

= 400kg x 0.5m/s^2

= **200N**

HT When body A exerts a force on body B, body B exerts an equal but opposite force on Body A. For example, the girl in the diagram below is standing on the ground. She is being pulled down to the ground by gravity, and the ground is pushing up with an equal force.

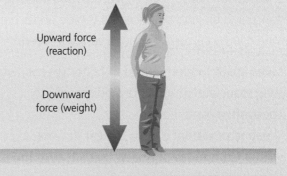

Upward force (reaction)

Downward force (weight)

Forces and Motion

Stopping Distance

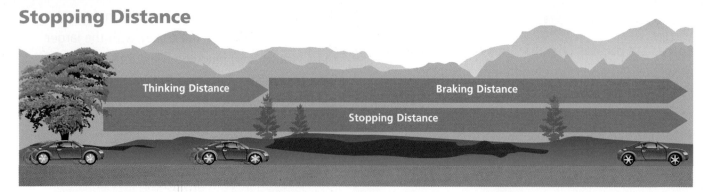

The **stopping** distance of a vehicle depends on...

- the **thinking** distance – the distance travelled by the vehicle from the point the driver realises he needs to brake to when he applies the brakes
- the **braking** distance – the distance travelled by the vehicle from the point the driver applies the brakes to the point at which the vehicle actually stops.

> **Stopping distance ═ Thinking distance ＋ Braking distance**

The thinking distance is increased if...

- the vehicle is travelling faster
- the driver is ill, tired or under the influence of alcohol or drugs
- the driver is distracted or is not fully concentrating
- there is poor visibility – this delays the time before the driver realises he needs to apply the brakes.

The braking distance is increased if...

- the vehicle is travelling faster
- there are poor weather / road conditions, e.g. if it is wet, slippery, icy
- the vehicle is in poor condition, e.g. brakes and tyres are worn out, tyres are not inflated properly.

The illustration above right shows how the thinking distance and braking distance of a vehicle under normal driving conditions depend on the vehicle's speed.

It takes much longer to stop at faster speeds, which is why road safety regulations advise you to...

- obey the speed limits
- keep your distance from the car in front
- allow extra room between cars, or drive more slowly in bad weather or poor road conditions.

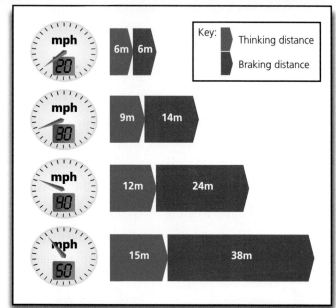

HT The braking distance of a vehicle is increased if...

- the **mass** of the vehicle is **increased** – a loaded vehicle, i.e. a vehicle with passengers, baggage, etc., has a greater kinetic energy, which increases the braking distance
- the **friction** between the tyres and the road is **decreased** – a wet or greasy road surface reduces the amount of friction between the tyres and the road, which increases the braking distance
- the **braking force** applied is **decreased** – a smaller force exerted by the brake pads on the wheel discs increases the braking distance
- the vehicle is **travelling faster** – a faster vehicle has greater kinetic energy which increases the braking distance.

Work

Work is done whenever a force moves an object. Every day you are doing **work** and developing **power**, for example…

- lifting weights
- climbing stairs
- pulling a wheelie bin
- pushing a shopping trolley.

Energy is needed to do work. Both energy and work are measured in joules, J. Therefore…

> **Work done (J) = Energy transferred (J)**

The amount of work done depends on…

- the **size** of the force in newtons
- the **distance** the object is moved in metres.

> **Work done (J) = Force (N) X Distance (m)**
>
> W
> ─────
> F x d

Example

A man pushes a car with a steady force of 250N. The car moves a distance of 20m. How much work does the man do?

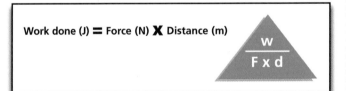

250N push ➡

Work done = Force x Distance

= 250N x 20m

= **5000J (or 5kJ)**

Power

Power is a measure of how quickly work is done, i.e. the work done per second. The unit of power is the **watt, W**.

Some cars have much higher **power ratings** than others and they may also use far more fuel. High fuel consumption is expensive for the driver and is also damaging to the environment.

Power, work done and time taken are linked by the following formula…

> Power (W) = $\dfrac{\text{Work done (J)}}{\text{Time (s)}}$
>
> W
> ─────
> P x t

Example 1

A girl does 2400 joules of work when she runs up a flight of stairs in 8 seconds. Calculate her power.

Power = $\dfrac{\text{Work done}}{\text{Time}}$

$= \dfrac{2400J}{8s}$

= **300W**

Example 2

A crane does 200 000J of work when it lifts a load of 25 000N. The power of the crane is 50kW.

a) Calculate the distance moved by the load. Rearrange the formula…

Distance = $\dfrac{\text{Work done}}{\text{Force}}$

$= \dfrac{200\,000J}{25\,000N}$

= **8m**

b) Calculate the time taken to move the load. Rearrange the formula…

Time = $\dfrac{\text{Work done}}{\text{Power}}$

$= \dfrac{200\,000J}{50\,000W}$ ⟵ Power must be in watts

= **4s**

Energy on the Move

Kinetic Energy

Kinetic energy is the energy an object has because of its movement, i.e. if it is moving it has got kinetic energy. The following all have kinetic energy:

- a ball rolling along the ground
- a car travelling along a road
- a boy running.

Kinetic energy depends on two things:

- the **mass** of the object (kg)
- the **speed** of the object (m/s).

A moving car has kinetic energy because it has both mass and speed. However…

- if the car moves with a greater speed it has more kinetic energy (providing its mass has not changed)

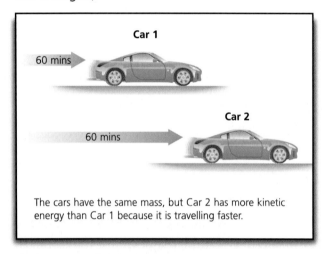

Car 1

60 mins

Car 2

60 mins

The cars have the same mass, but Car 2 has more kinetic energy than Car 1 because it is travelling faster.

- if the mass of the car is greater (e.g. there are more people inside it, or it is a larger vehicle, e.g. a truck) it may have more kinetic energy, even if its speed is less than that of another car.

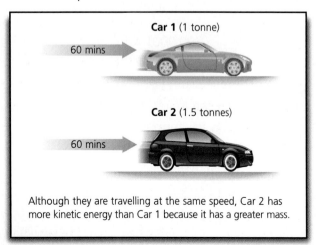

Car 1 (1 tonne)

60 mins

Car 2 (1.5 tonnes)

60 mins

Although they are travelling at the same speed, Car 2 has more kinetic energy than Car 1 because it has a greater mass.

Although most cars rely on **fossil fuels** such as **petrol** or **diesel** for their energy, **electricity** can also be used. **Battery-driven** cars are already on our roads and **solar-powered** cars will soon follow.

Unlike cars powered by fossil fuels, cars powered by electricity do not pollute at the point of use. However, their batteries are recharged using electricity that is generated in power stations, which cause pollution.

> **HT** The formula for calculating kinetic energy is…
>
> $$\text{Kinetic energy (J)} = \frac{1}{2} \times \text{Mass (kg)} \times \text{Speed}^2 \text{ (m/s)}^2$$
>
> KE
> $$\frac{1}{2} \times m \times v^2$$
>
> where v is speed

Example 1

A car of mass 1000kg is moving at a speed of 10m/s. How much kinetic energy does it have?

Use the formula…

$$\text{Kinetic energy (J)} = \frac{1}{2} \times \text{Mass (kg)} \times \text{Speed}^2 \text{ (m/s)}^2$$

$$= \frac{1}{2} \times 1000\text{kg} \times (10\text{m/s})^2$$

$$= \textbf{50 000J (or 50kJ)}$$

Example 2

Calculate the kinetic energy of a toy car of mass 400g moving at a speed of 0.5m/s.

Use the formula…

$$\text{Kinetic energy (J)} = \frac{1}{2} \times \text{Mass (kg)} \times \text{Speed}^2 \text{ (m/s)}^2$$

$$= \frac{1}{2} \times 0.4\text{kg} \times (0.5\text{m/s})^2$$

$$= \textbf{0.05J}$$

> Mass must be in kg:
> $$\frac{400\text{g}}{1000} = 0.4\text{kg}$$

Fuel Consumption

Car **fuel consumption** depends upon…

- the energy required to increase the **kinetic energy**
- the energy required to work against friction
- driving style and speed
- road conditions.

Crumple Zones

Car Safety Features

Modern cars have **safety features** that **absorb energy** on collision, including…

- **seatbelts** – to prevent the people in the car from being propelled out of the windscreen if the car comes to a sudden halt
- **air bags** – to cushion the impact for the driver and front passenger
- **brakes** – to reduce the speed of the car by transferring kinetic energy to heat energy
- **crumple zone** – a region of the car designed specifically to 'crumple' during a collision. This absorbs a lot of the energy in a crash, reducing the danger to the people in the car.

Crumple zones, seatbelts and air bags all **change shape** on impact to **absorb energy** and therefore reduce the risk of injury to the people in the car.

Seatbelts have to be replaced after a crash because they can be damaged by the forces they experience.

Crumple zone

Active Safety Features

Active safety features on a car are there to help you escape from, or protect you during, **a crash situation**, for example…

- **anti-lock braking systems** (ABS) – prevent the tyres from skidding, which means the vehicle stops more quickly and allows the driver to remain in control of the steering
- **traction control** – prevents the car from skidding while accelerating, so the driver can quickly escape from a dangerous situation
- **safety cage** – metal cage which strengthens the cabin section of the car to prevent the vehicle from collapsing when upside down or rolling.

Safety Cage Reinforces Body of Car

Passive Safety Features

Passive safety features are there to help **prevent an accident** by reducing distractions, for example…

- **electric windows** make it easier for the driver to open or close the windows whilst driving, causing less of a distraction
- **cruise control** allows the driver to select a speed that the car automatically sticks to. This helps reduce accidental speeding
- **paddle shift controls** allow the driver to keep both hands on the steering wheel when changing gear and adjusting the stereo
- **adjustable seating** allows all drivers to obtain a comfortable position in which they can reach the steering wheel and control pedals easily.

HT Reducing Stopping Forces

The stopping **forces** experienced by the people in the car in a collision can be reduced by…
- increasing the stopping or collision time
- increasing the stopping or collision distance
- decelerating.

All of the safety features mentioned on the left of this page perform one or more of the above tasks. By reducing the stopping forces on the people in the car, they reduce the risk of injury.

Anti-lock braking systems prevent the tyres from skidding which increases the area of the tyres that is in contact with the road. This increases the friction between the two surfaces. Friction is a force which opposes the direction of travel, therefore, the car is able to stop more quickly.

Falling Safely

Terminal Speed

Falling objects experience two forces (see diagram opposite):

- the downward force of **weight**, W (↓) which always stays the same
- the upward force of **air resistance**, R or drag (↑).

Weight and Gravity

Objects **fall** because of their **weight** and they get faster as they fall. Weight is a **force** pulling us towards the centre of the planet, in our case, Earth. The strength of this force depends upon the **gravity** of the planet.

Friction and Air Resistance

Frictional forces, such as **drag**, **friction** and **air resistance**, can act against the movement of the object, slowing it down. This effect can be reduced by...

- changing the **shape** (e.g. to increase or decrease air resistance)
- using a **lubricant** (to make the object slide through the air with less resistance).

The **shape** of an object can influence its top speed...

- **shuttlecocks** in badminton are designed to increase air resistance so they travel slower
- **parachutes** are designed to have a larger surface area to increase air resistance
- **roof boxes** on cars may provide useful luggage space but they increase air resistance
- **deflectors** on lorries and caravans will reduce air resistance
- **sports cars** are wedge-shaped to reduce air resistance.

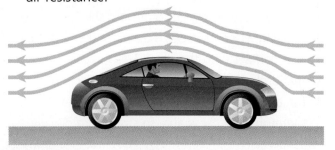

When a skydiver jumps out of an aeroplane, the speed of his descent can be considered in two separate parts: before his parachute opens (i.e. when the skydiver is in free-fall) and after his parachute opens (when his air resistance is greatly increased due to the surface area of his parachute).

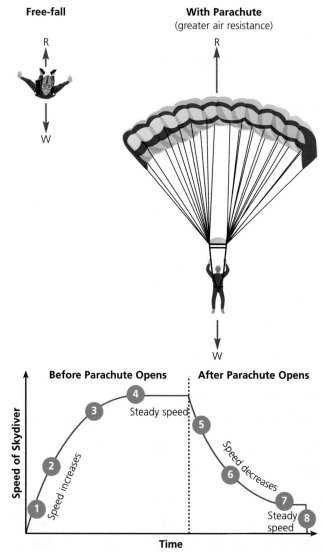

When there is **no atmosphere**, falling objects do not experience drag and their **acceleration** in free-fall is **constant**. This is the case on the moon and elsewhere in space.

> **HT** At higher speeds, falling objects experience more drag. If you increase the area of the object that is facing downwards, you increase the drag. The terminal speed occurs when the drag is equal to the weight of the object.

The Motion of a Skydiver

Before the Parachute Opens

When the skydiver jumps, he initially accelerates due to the force of gravity (see **①**).

Gravity is a force of attraction that acts between bodies that have mass, e.g. the skydiver and the Earth.

The **weight** of an object is the force exerted on it by gravity. It is measured in newtons (N).

As the skydiver falls he experiences the frictional force of air resistance (R) in the opposite direction. But this is not as great as W so he continues to accelerate (see **②**).

As his speed increases, so does the air resistance acting on him (see **③**), until eventually R is equal to W (see **④**).

This means that the force acting on him is now zero and his falling speed becomes constant. This speed is called the **terminal speed**.

After the Parachute Opens

When the parachute is opened, unbalanced forces act again because the upward force of R is now greatly increased and is bigger than W (see **⑤**).

This increased force of R decreases his speed, and as his speed decreases so does R (see **⑥**).

Eventually R decreases until it is equal to W (see **⑦**). The forces acting are once again balanced and for the second time he falls at a steady speed.

However, this time it is slower than before, i.e. at a new terminal speed.

Balanced forces and therefore constant speed

Balanced forces and therefore constant speed

The Energy of Games and Theme Rides

Gravitational Potential Energy

Gravitational potential energy is the energy that is stored in an object due to its position in the Earth's gravitational field. If an object can fall it has got gravitational potential energy, e.g. a diver standing on a diving board (before he jumps off).

A man standing on a higher diving board will have more gravitational potential energy than another man standing on a lower diving board (providing they have the same mass) because he is further away from the ground (see diagram ❶).

A heavier man standing on the same diving board as a lighter man will have more gravitational potential energy because he has a bigger mass (see diagram ❷).

When an object falls it converts gravitational potential energy into kinetic energy. This is what happens when...

• the diver jumps off the diving board
• a ball rolls down a hill
• a skydiver jumps out of a plane.

> **HT** The formula for gravitational potential energy is:
>
> $$\text{Gravitational potential energy (J)} = \text{Mass (kg)} \times \text{Gravitational field strength (N/kg)} \times \text{Vertical height (m)}$$
>
> $$\frac{\text{GPE}}{\text{m} \times \text{g} \times \text{h}}$$

HT Gravitational field strength, g, is a constant. On Earth it has a value of 10N/kg. This means that every 1kg of matter near the surface of the Earth experiences a downwards force of 10N due to gravity.

On planets where the gravitational field strength is higher, the gravitational potential energy is greater.

Example 1
A skier of mass 80kg gets on a ski lift which takes her from a height of 1000m to a height of 3000m above ground. By how much does her gravitational potential energy increase?

Use the formula...

$$\text{Gravitational potential energy (J)} = \text{Mass (kg)} \times \text{Gravitational field strength (N/kg)} \times \text{Vertical height (m)}$$

= 80kg x 10N/kg x (3000m – 1000m)
= 80kg x 10N/kg x 2000m
= 1 600 000J (or 1600kJ)

The skier was already at a height of 1000m

N.B. Work has been done by the ski lift motor so that the skier can increase her gravitational potential energy. In other words, work done by the motor has been transferred into gravitational potential energy.

Example 2
A ball is kicked vertically upwards from the ground. Its mass is 0.2kg and it increases its gravitational potential energy by 30J when it reaches the top point in its flight. What height does the ball reach?

Rearrange the formula...

$$\text{Vertical height} = \frac{\text{GPE}}{\text{Mass x Gravitational field strength}}$$

$$= \frac{30J}{0.2kg \times 10N/kg}$$

= 15m

The Energy of Games and Theme Rides

Gravitational Potential Energy and Kinetic Energy

When an object falls, its gravitational potential energy is transferred to kinetic energy. There are many theme park rides which use this transfer of energy.

1 On most roller-coasters, the cars start high up with a lot of gravitational potential energy.

2 As the cars drop, the gravitational potential energy is gradually transferred into kinetic energy.

3 The car reaches its highest speed, maximum kinetic energy, at the bottom of the slope.

4 As the car climbs the slope on the other side, kinetic energy is converted back into gravitational potential energy.

If the **mass** of the car is **doubled**, the **kinetic energy** also **doubles**.

If the **speed** of the car is **doubled**, the **kinetic energy quadruples**.

Increasing the **gravitational field strength**, **g**, will increase the gravitational potential energy, but this would require you to move the roller-coaster to a different planet!

> **HT** When an object is travelling at its terminal speed, the speed is not changing so the kinetic energy does not increase. However, the gravitational potential energy decreases as the object does work against friction (gravitational potential energy is transferred into heat and sound energy).

HT Weight and Mass

Weight is due to the force of gravity on an object. The mass of an object is the amount of matter that it contains. The weight of an object and its mass are linked by two related formulae:

Weight (N)	=	Mass (kg)	X	Acceleration of free-fall (m/s²)	$\frac{W}{m \times g}$
Weight (N)	=	Mass (kg)	X	Gravitational field strength (N/kg)	$\frac{W}{m \times g}$

If there is no air resistance acting, then a falling object near the Earth's surface has an acceleration of 10m/s^2 which is known as the acceleration of free-fall, g. The force which causes this acceleration is the weight of the object. In principle, this formula is the same as F = ma.

Example

Calculate the weight of a falling stone of mass 0.1kg if $g = 10 \text{m/s}^2$.

Use the formula…
Weight = Mass x Acceleration of free-fall
$= 0.1 \text{kg} \times 10 \text{m/s}^2 = \textbf{1N}$

Near the surface of the Earth the gravitational field strength, g, is 10N/kg which means that every 1kg of matter experiences a downwards force, or has a weight, of 10N.

Example

Calculate the weight of a stone of mass 0.1kg on Earth if g is 10N/kg.

Use the formula…
Weight = Mass x Gravitational field strength
$= 0.1 \text{kg} \times 10 \text{N/kg} = \textbf{1N}$

N.B. Acceleration of free-fall and gravitational field strength are numerically the same, i.e 10m/s^2 and 10N/kg. They also both have the same symbol, g. In your exam you may be given questions on either.

Who Planted That There?

Leaves

The leaves are the food 'factories' of the plant, and nearly all **photosynthesis** occurs there. They are specially adapted to be super-efficient. Some of the leaf's adaptations are listed below:

- it contains **chlorophyll** (which absorbs light) in millions of **chloroplasts**
- it is broad and flat to provide a **huge surface area** to absorb sunlight for photosynthesis
- it has a **network of veins** to transport water to the cells and remove the products of photosynthesis, i.e. glucose
- it has a **thin structure** so the gases (carbon dioxide and oxygen) only have a short distance to travel to and from the cells
- it has **stomata** (tiny pores) on the underside of the leaf to allow carbon dioxide and oxygen to diffuse in and out for photosynthesis and respiration.

The carbon dioxide needed for photosynthesis **diffuses** in through the stomata. The oxygen produced by photosynthesis diffuses out.

The diagram below shows a section of a typical leaf. The structure is made up of four distinct layers: the upper epidermis, the palisade layer, the spongy mesophyll and the lower epidermis.

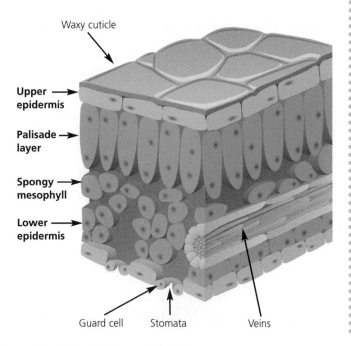

Waxy cuticle

Upper epidermis

Palisade layer

Spongy mesophyll

Lower epidermis

Guard cell Stomata Veins

The diagram (below opposite) shows a section of a typical leaf:

- the waxy cuticle restricts water loss from the leaf
- the upper epidermis is transparent to allow sunlight through to the layer below
- the cells in the palisade layer are positioned near the top of the leaf to absorb the maximum amount of light and are packed with chloroplasts (see diagram below) which absorb the light energy needed for photosynthesis
- the spongy mesophyll contains lots of air spaces connected to the stomata to ensure the optimum exchange of gases
- the lower epidermis contains most of the stomata
- stomata allow the diffusion of gases (i.e. carbon dioxide and oxygen) in and out of the leaf
- guard cells control the size of the stomata to restrict water loss
- veins contain xylem and phloem to transport water and sugars through the leaf.

This structure provides a very large surface area to volume ratio for efficient gaseous exchange, i.e. the absorption of carbon dioxide and the release of oxygen during photosynthesis.

A Palisade Cell

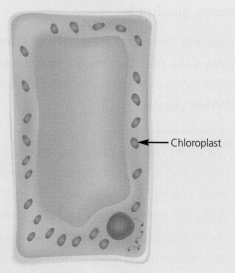

Chloroplast

Water, Water Everywhere

Osmosis

Osmosis is the diffusion of water from a dilute solution to a more concentrated solution through a partially permeable membrane (a membrane that allows the passage of water molecules but not solute molecules). In other words, water diffuses from a region where it is in a high concentration (i.e. a dilute solution) to where it is in a low concentration (i.e. a concentrated solution).

Water moves from a cell that contains a lot of water to a cell that contains less water (see diagram ❶) so there is the same amount of water in each cell (see diagram ❷).

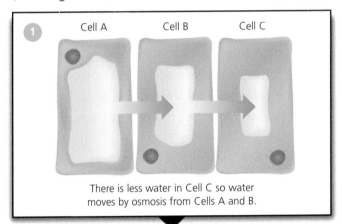

There is less water in Cell C so water moves by osmosis from Cells A and B.

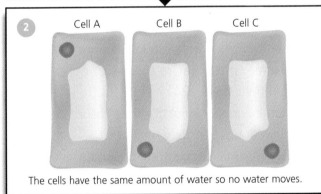

The cells have the same amount of water so no water moves.

The cell walls do not affect the movement of water or dissolved substances. The cell membranes allow the movement of water but not the movement of dissolved substances.

Both osmosis and diffusion involve the movement of molecules from a high concentration to a low concentration. They differ in that osmosis is the movement of water molecules, and diffusion is the movement of other substances.

More on Osmosis

When predicting the direction of water movement, the only thing that matters is the concentration of the water because the solute molecules cannot pass through the membrane, only the water molecules can.

The water particles move randomly, colliding with each other and passing through the membrane in both directions. Overall, however, more particles move from the area where water is in high concentration to low concentration (see diagram below); the net movement of molecules is from the region of high concentration to the region of low concentration. The effect is to gradually dilute the solution.

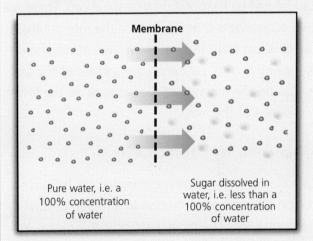

Pure water, i.e. a 100% concentration of water

Sugar dissolved in water, i.e. less than a 100% concentration of water

At the root hair cells, water gradually moves from the soil into the cell by osmosis along a concentration gradient.

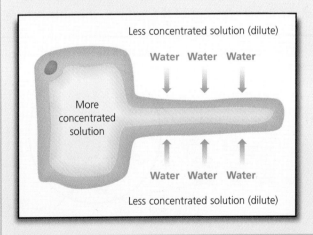

Less concentrated solution (dilute)

Water Water Water

More concentrated solution

Water Water Water

Less concentrated solution (dilute)

Water, Water Everywhere

Water in Plants

Plants use water to…
- keep their leaves cool
- transport minerals
- enable them to photosynthesise to produce glucose
- keep cells firm and therefore keep the plant rigid.

Plants need to balance the amount of water they take in with the amount of water they lose. Water is taken into the plant via the roots, which are specially adapted to increase their ability to take in water by having root hair cells. These cells increase the surface area of the root, making a greater area for absorption.

The water then travels through the plant up to the leaves, along a concentration gradient from an area of high concentration of water to an area of low concentration of water. When it reaches the leaves it can be lost by evaporation (transpiration). There are two adaptations that can reduce the rate at which water is lost from the leaves into the atmosphere:
- having a waxy cuticle on the surface of the leaf
- having the majority of the stomata on the lower surface of the leaf.

Osmosis in Plant Cells

Diffusion is the movement of molecules from a region of high concentration to a region of low concentration. The movement of water molecules by diffusion is known as **osmosis**.

In a leaf, water moves out of the cell by osmosis and into the spaces in the spongy mesophyll layer from where it will pass out of the leaf into the atmosphere.

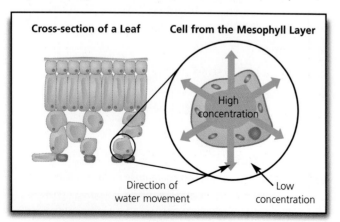

Cross-section of a Leaf   Cell from the Mesophyll Layer

High concentration

Direction of water movement   Low concentration

Maintaining Support

Plant cells have inelastic cell walls which, together with the water inside the cells, are essential for the support of young non-woody plants. The cell wall prevents cells from bursting due to excess water entering them and, at the same time, contributes to rigidity.

A lack of water can cause plants to wilt. As the amount of water inside the cells reduces, the cells become less rigid due to reduced pressure.

If there is plenty of water in the soil, stomata open to allow transpiration and the diffusion of gases. The plant cells will be full of water so the plant stays erect. This is the main method of support for young plants.

When there is not enough water available in the soil, stomata close to try to prevent transpiration and the diffusion of gases, so photosynthesis has to stop. The plant cells are short of water so they are not strong, which causes the plant to wilt.

Osmosis in Animal Cells

Water also diffuses in and out of animal cells by osmosis. The difference here is that animal cells do not have a cell wall, so if too much water enters a cell, it could burst.

1. When red blood cells are in solutions which are the same concentration as their cytoplasm they retain their shape.
2. When in weaker solution, they absorb water and swell up, and they may burst.
3. When in more concentrated solution, they lose water and shrivel up.

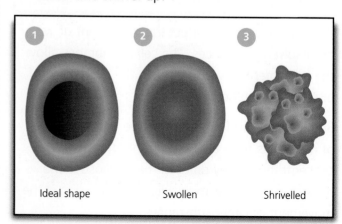

Ideal shape   Swollen   Shrivelled

Turgor Pressure

When water moves into plant cells by osmosis it increases the pressure inside the cell. (This is rather like blowing up a balloon inside a cereal carton.) However, the cell walls are sufficiently strong to withstand the pressure and as a result the cell becomes very rigid. This is called **turgor pressure**. Cells that have sufficient supplies of water are described as maintaining their turgor, i.e. staying rigid.

When all the cells are fully turgid the plant is rigid and upright. However, if water is in short supply, cells will start to lose water by osmosis. They lose turgor pressure and become flaccid, and the plant begins to wilt. If the cells lose a lot of water, the inside of the cells contract like a deflating balloon. This is called **plasmolysis**.

Water Loss from Leaves

Transpiration and water loss are an unavoidable consequence of photosynthesis. The leaf consists of moist cells exposed to the atmosphere via the stomata, which can be found on the under surface of the leaf. A lot of stomata are needed as they allow the exchange of gases during photosynthesis, but they also allow water molecules to pass out of the leaf. The number, position, size and distribution of stomata vary between plants, depending on the environment they live in and, therefore, the amount of water they require.

The leaf is adapted to be able to reduce water loss. The turgidity of guard cells changes in relation to the light intensity and availability of water in order to regulate the size of the stomatal openings.

When a plant is exposed to sunlight and a sufficient supply of water, photosynthesis occurs in the cells of its leaves, including the guard cells. Photosynthesis produces glucose and this creates a concentration gradient so that water enters them via osmosis. This makes the guard cells turgid and the stomata fully open allowing the exchange of gases and water loss. When there is insufficient water, the guard cells become flaccid and the stomata close. This prevents unnecessary water loss but also prevents photosynthesis because carbon dioxide cannot get in.

- High light-intensity causes the stomata to open which increases the rate of evaporation of water from the leaf.
- High temperatures increase the movement of the water molecules and so speed up transpiration out of the leaf.
- Increased air movement blows the water molecules away from the stomata which increases transpiration.
- High humidity decreases the concentration gradient and so slows down transpiration.

More on Osmosis in Animals

The cytoplasm of a red blood cell has the same water concentration as plasma. There is no net movement of water into or out of the cell, so it can maintain its biconcave shape.

If blood cells are put into pure water, they gain lots of water by osmosis. There is nothing to prevent the water entering the cell so they eventually burst. This is called **lysis**.

Blood cells in a concentrated solution (very little water) lose water by osmosis. They shrivel up and become **crenated** (have scalloped edges).

The different behaviour of animal and plant cells in response to osmosis is because animal cells do not have a cell wall. When plant cells absorb water they expand but resistance from the cell wall eventually stops them from absorbing any more water and bursting. Animal cells do not have a cell wall so they absorb more and more water until lysis occurs.

Transport in Plants

The Structure of a Plant

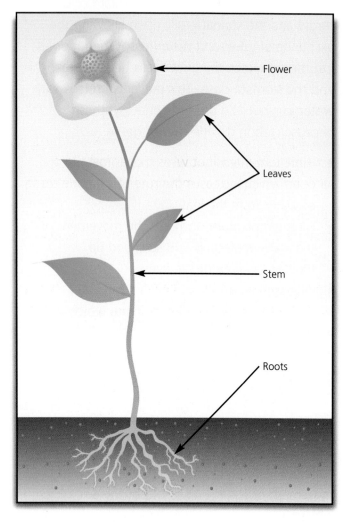

Flower

The flower contains the reproductive organs of the plant, which are required to make seeds.

Leaves

Leaves are broad, thin and flat to provide a large surface area to absorb sunlight, which is needed for photosynthesis.

Stem

In most plants, the stem supports the plant and transports substances from the roots to the leaves by the transport tissues: xylem and phloem.

Xylem transport water and soluble mineral salts from the roots to the leaves (transpiration) to replace water lost by transpiration and photosynthesis.

Phloem allow the movement of food substances around the plant (translocation).

The xylem and phloem form a continuous system of tubes from roots to leaves. The diagram below shows how xylem and phloem are arranged in the stem:

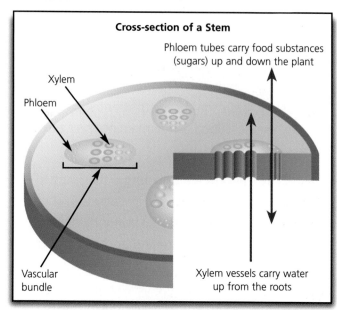

Transpiration is the evaporation and diffusion of water from inside leaves. The transpiration stream is powered by the evaporation of water from the leaf:

1. Water evaporates from the internal leaf cells through the stomata.
2. Water passes by osmosis from the xylem vessels to leaf cells, which pulls the entire thread of water in that vessel upwards by a very small amount.
3. Water enters the xylem from root tissue to replace water which has moved upwards.
4. Water enters root hair cells by osmosis to replace water which has entered the xylem.

> **HT** Xylem vessels are hollow tubes made from dead plant cells. The cellulose cell walls are thickened and strengthened with a waterproof substance.
>
> Phloem cells are long columns of living cells, able to translocate (move) sugars both up and down the plant.

Roots

Roots anchor the plant firmly in the ground and absorb water. The root hair cells have an enormous surface area for absorption of water.

Factors Affecting the Rate of Transpiration

The rate that water evaporates from the leaves of a plant is affected by the external conditions. The factors that affect the rate of transpiration are…

- **light** – more light increases the rate of photosynthesis and therefore also increases the transpiration rate
- **air movement** (wind) – transpiration increases as the movement of the air increases
- **heat** – the rate of photosynthesis increases as heat increases, and this increases the rate of transpiration as a result
- **humidity** – humidity decreases the rate of transpiration.

A leafy shoot's rate of transpiration can be measured using a potometer (see diagram below).

The shoot is held in a test tube with a bung around the top to prevent any water from evaporating (this would give a false measurement of the water lost by transpiration).

As the plant transpires, it takes up water from the test tube to replace that which it has lost. All the water is then pulled up, moving the air bubble along.

The distance the air bubble moves can be used to calculate the plant's rate of transpiration for a given time period.

The experiment can be repeated, varying a different factor each time, to see how each factor affects the rate of transpiration.

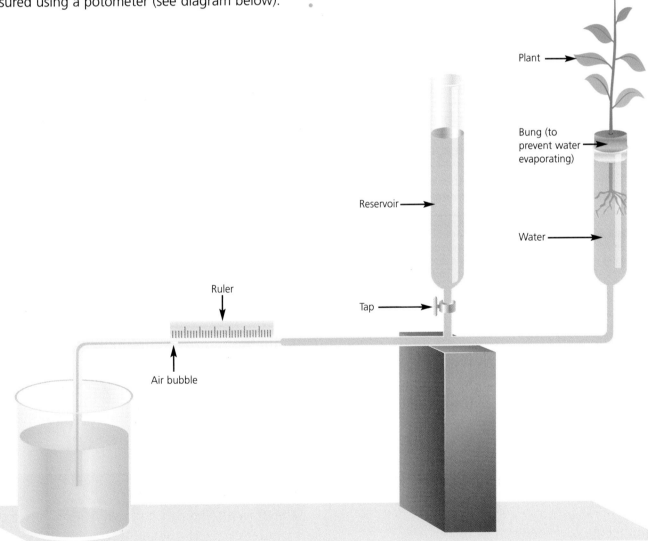

Plant

Bung (to prevent water evaporating)

Reservoir

Water

Ruler

Tap

Air bubble

Plants Need Minerals Too

Essential Minerals

Essential minerals – nitrates, potassium, phosphates and magnesium – are needed in order to make proteins and other compounds to keep the plant healthy and growing properly. Plants absorb these essential minerals through their root hairs as ions dissolved in water.

The minerals are naturally present in the soil but they are usually in quite low concentrations. Therefore, farmers use fertilisers, which contain essential minerals, to ensure the plants get all the minerals they need.

Each mineral is needed for a different purpose (see table below).

If one or more of the essential minerals is missing from the soil, the growth of the plant will be affected (see diagrams below).

Active Transport

Substances are sometimes absorbed against a concentration gradient, i.e. from a low to a high concentration. This is the opposite direction to which normal diffusion occurs. This is called active transport and it requires energy from respiration in the same way that pulling a trolley up a hill would require energy. Plants absorb ions from very dilute solutions, i.e. actively (see below).

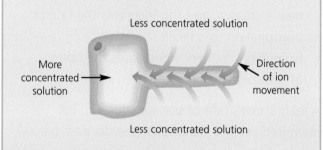

Less concentrated solution

More concentrated solution

Direction of ion movement

Less concentrated solution

Mineral	Why it is Needed	How it is Used
Nitrates	To make proteins for cell growth.	To make amino acids that form the proteins.
Potassium	For respiration and photosynthesis.	To help the enzymes in these processes.
Phosphates	For respiration and cell growth.	To make DNA and cell membranes.
Magnesium	For photosynthesis.	To make the chlorophyll for photosynthesis.

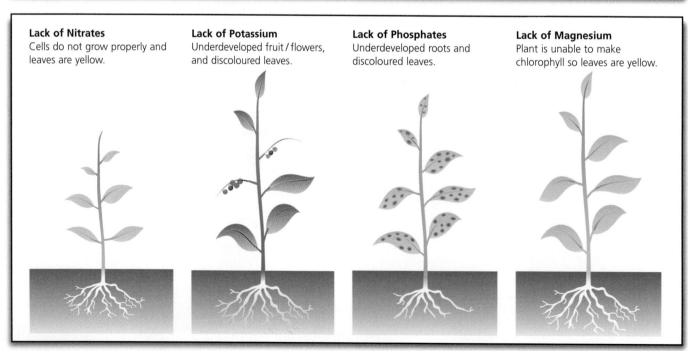

Lack of Nitrates
Cells do not grow properly and leaves are yellow.

Lack of Potassium
Underdeveloped fruit / flowers, and discoloured leaves.

Lack of Phosphates
Underdeveloped roots and discoloured leaves.

Lack of Magnesium
Plant is unable to make chlorophyll so leaves are yellow.

Food Chains

Food chains show which organisms consume (eat) which other organisms. They also show the transfer of energy and materials from organism to organism. Energy from the Sun enters the food chain when green plants absorb sunlight in order to photosynthesise. Feeding passes this energy, and biomass (living material), from one organism to the next along the food chain.

Green plants are known as **producers** because they produce biomass when they photosynthesise.

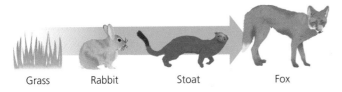

Grass   Rabbit   Stoat   Fox

The arrow shows the flow of energy and biomass along the food chain.

- All food chains start with a green plant called the **producer**.
- The rabbit is a herbivore (plant eater) and the **primary consumer**.
- The stoat is a carnivore (meat eater) and the **secondary consumer**.
- The fox is the top carnivore and the **tertiary consumer**.

Pyramid of Numbers

The number of organisms at each level in the food chain can be shown as a pyramid of numbers.

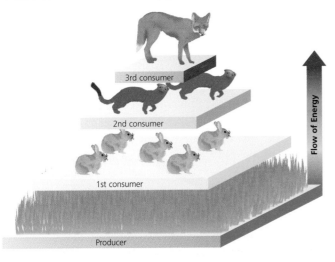

As we go up from one level to the next, the number of organisms decreases quite dramatically: a lot of grass feeds a few rabbits, which feeds even fewer stoats, which feed just one fox.

This is because at each stage of the food chain energy is lost as heat (during respiration) and via egestion (removal of undigested food).

For simplicity, pyramids of numbers usually look like this:

Pyramids of numbers do not take into account the mass of the organisms, so it is possible to end up with some odd-looking pyramids. Look at the following example:

Because lots of slugs feed on one lettuce, the base of the pyramid is smaller than the next stage. This happens because the lettuce is a large organism compared to the slug. This situation also happens when trees are at the start of a food chain.

Pyramid of Biomass

Pyramids of biomass deal with the mass of living material in the chain. They are always pyramid shaped because they take the mass of the organisms into account. The food pyramid above would give:

If enough information is given, the pyramid of biomass can be drawn to scale.

Energy Flow

Transfer of Energy and Biomass

Biomass and energy are lost at every stage (trophic level) of a food chain because…

- materials and energy are lost in an organism's faeces during egestion
- energy is 'lost' through movement and respiration.

The last statement is particularly true of warm-blooded animals (birds and mammals).

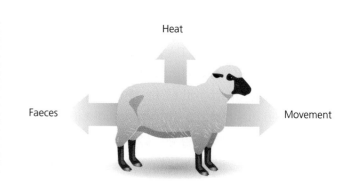

Efficiency of Energy Transfer

If we know how much energy is stored in the living organisms at each level of a food chain, the efficiency of energy transfer can be calculated by dividing the amount of energy used usefully (e.g. for growth) by the total amount of energy taken in:

$$\text{Energy efficiency (\%)} = \frac{\text{Energy used usefully}}{\text{Total energy taken in}} \times 100$$

Example

A sheep eats 100kJ of energy in the form of grass but only 5kJ becomes new body tissue; the rest is lost as faeces, urine or heat. Calculate the efficiency of energy transfer in the sheep:

$$\text{Energy efficiency} = \frac{5}{100} \times 100$$

$$= 5\%$$

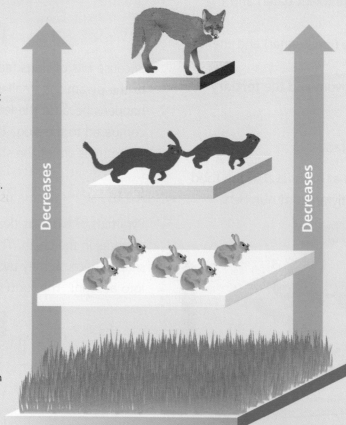

Energy

The fox gets the last tiny bit of energy left after all the others have had a share. This explains why food chains rarely have fourth degree or fifth degree consumers – they would not get enough energy.

The stoats run around, mate, excrete, keep warm, etc. and pass on about a tenth of all the energy they get from the rabbits.

The rabbits run around, mate, excrete, keep warm, etc. and pass on about a tenth of all the energy they get from the grass.

The Sun is the energy source for all organisms, but only a fraction of the Sun's energy is captured in photosynthesis.

Biomass

The fox gets the remaining biomass.

The stoats lose quite a bit of biomass in faeces and urine.

The rabbits lose quite a lot of biomass in faeces and urine.

A lot of the biomass remains in the ground as the root system.

Biomass

Plants use some of the glucose from photosynthesis to produce starch and cellulose which they use to grow plant tissues. This new plant material is biomass.

Fuels from Biomass

Biomass can be burned to release energy, so it can be used as a fuel. Some examples of biomass that can be used as fuels are…

- fast-growing trees, e.g. pine – can be burned to release energy

- manure or other waste – can be broken down by bacteria in a fermenter to release methane (biogas) which can be used to power electricity generators

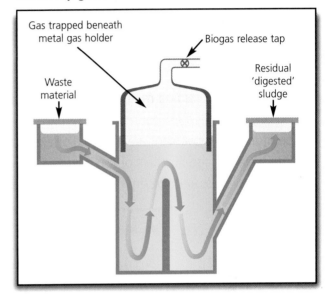

- corn or sugar cane – can be broken down by yeast in a fermenter to produce alcohol. Bio-ethanol (made in a similar way) can be used to fuel some cars.

Advantages of Biofuels

- Biofuels are renewable – plants can be grown quickly and easily, unlike fossil fuels, e.g. oil and coal, which cannot be replaced in a lifetime and will eventually run out.
- Biofuels are cleaner than fossil fuels – they produce much less air pollution when burned. Also, the plants grown to make biofuels use up the CO_2 made when the biofuels are burned. So, overall, less CO_2 goes into the atmosphere, reducing the greenhouse effect.
- Countries can produce their own biofuel and are not dependent on oil-producing countries for their energy supplies.

More Uses of Biomass

A crop like maize (corn) produces a lot of biomass which can be used for…
- feed for livestock
- food for humans
- biofuel (after being fermented)
- seeds to grow more biomass.

Farming

Intensive Farming

Farmers are increasingly faced with the challenge of producing higher yields of food at lower costs. To achieve this, they can use intensive farming practices to produce as much food as possible from the available land, plants and animals. Pesticides, insecticides and herbicides are used in this process.

Intensive farming practices include keeping animals in carefully controlled environments where their temperature and movement are limited. For example, fish farms breed huge numbers of fish in enclosed nets in the sea or lakes, and battery farms raise chickens in cages. However, this can raise ethical dilemmas: some people find this morally unacceptable because the animals have a poor quality of life.

Pesticides are used to kill pests that can damage crops or farm animals. Great care needs to be taken with pesticides as they can harm other organisms (non-pests) and build up (accumulate) in food chains, harming animals at the top.

Insecticides are used to kill insect pests; fungicides are used to kill fungi; and herbicides are used to kill weeds which would compete with the crop for water and nutrients.

Accumulation of Pesticides

Herbicides and pesticides reduce the weeds and pests and, therefore, the energy that is taken by competing plants and pests. However, they can cause problems. Pesticides can flow into rivers where they can be absorbed by algae (tiny plants). The algae is eaten by small aquatic organisms, which in turn are eaten by larger organisms.

The pesticide increases in concentration along the food chain. So, while the pesticide may not damage the algae or the smaller organisms, the effect of the accumulation could easily kill the larger organisms.

The accumulation of pesticides can be shown by the following example (see diagram below)…

1. each tiny plant absorbs 2 units of pesticide
2. a small fish eats five plants – it has eaten
   5 x 2 = 10 units of pesticide
3. a bird eats four fish – it has eaten
   4 x 10 = 40 units of pesticide.

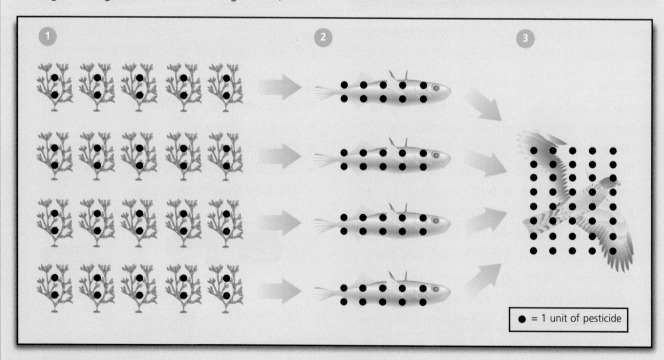

● = 1 unit of pesticide

Organic Farming

Some people have become very concerned about the impact of intensive farming on the quality of food produced, the welfare of animals, and the environment.

Organic farmers use various techniques to ensure that the quality of the food they produce is as high as possible, whilst maintaining the welfare of their animals and minimising the impact on the environment by...

- using animal manure or compost instead of chemical fertilisers
- growing nitrogen-fixing crops such as peas or clover to trap nitrogen into the soil
- rotating their crops to maintain soil fertility
- avoiding chemical pesticides by weeding and using biological controls (see p.66)
- varying seed planting times to discourage pests.

HT The table below gives some of the advantages and disadvantages of organic farming.

Advantages
• Food crops and the environment are not contaminated with artificial fertilisers or pesticides.
• Soil fertility is maintained through the use of organic fertilisers, and soil erosion is limited.
• Biodiversity in the local environment is promoted because hedgerows and other habitats are conserved.
• Livestock have space to roam.

Disadvantages
• Organic farming is less efficient because some crops are lost to pests and diseases.
• Organic fertiliser takes time to rot and does not supply a specific balance of minerals.

Hydroponics

Hydroponics is the term given to growing plants without soil. The plants grow with their roots in a solution. Minerals needed for healthy plant growth are added to the solution. Plants can be grown in greenhouses without soil using this system and it is also useful in areas where the soil is very thin or barren.

Certain plants, e.g. tomatoes, can be grown hydroponically in greenhouses. The temperature can be controlled using heaters; the light intensity can be controlled using lamps; and the carbon dioxide concentration can be controlled using chemicals; or as a by-product of the heaters.

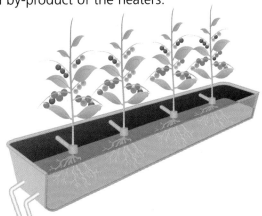

HT The table below gives some of the advantages and disadvantages of hydroponics:

Advantages
• The mineral levels added to the solution can be carefully controlled and adjusted to the type of plant.
• There is a reduced risk of the plants becoming diseased.

Disadvantages
• The plants have to be supported as they have no anchorage for their roots.
• Expensive fertilisers are a compulsory part of the system to supply the plant with minerals.

Farming

Biological Control

Instead of using pesticides, some farmers prefer to introduce a predator to reduce the number of pests. This is called **biological control**. For example, the cottony cushion scale (an insect) was a pest that attacked citrus fruit crops in America. However, when farmers introduced the ladybird beetle, the pest's numbers were significantly reduced.

Another example is the prickly pear cactus. It grew at a very fast rate and was taking over a lot of useful farm land, so a moth whose larva fed on the cactus' tissues was introduced, which reduced the number of cacti.

However, it is important to remember that whether biological control or pesticides are used to get rid of pests, thought must be given to the effect on the rest of the organisms in the food chain or web (see example below).

The table below lists the advantages and disadvantages of biological control.

Advantages
• The predator selected only usually attacks the pest, i.e. it is species-specific.
• Once the predator is introduced, it can have an impact over many years.
• The pest cannot become resistant to the predator (as it can to pesticides).

Disadvantages
• A great deal of time, research and cost is involved in developing control agents.
• Only about one-fifth of the biological controls are totally successful.
• The pest is not eliminated; it only has its numbers reduced.

Food Web

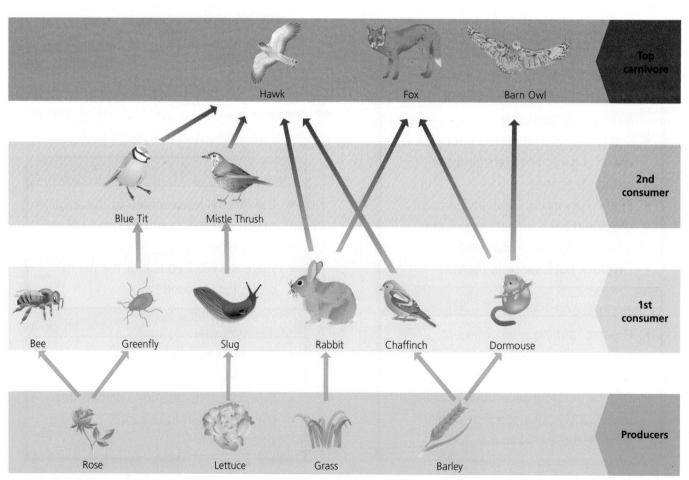

66

Decay

Decay is a process involving the breakdown of complex substances into simpler ones by microorganisms. The rate at which microorganisms break down substances is affected by several factors:

- **Temperature** – microorganisms responsible for decay work at their optimum at 40°C. Below this temperature; the microorganisms work slower; above this temperature they are denatured, which means they cannot carry out reactions.
- **Amount of oxygen** – microorganisms' rate of activity increases as the amount of oxygen in the air increases. So, generally, the more oxygen there is, the better.
- **Amount of water** – microorganisms prefer moist conditions. If there is too much water, the surroundings cool down, reducing the temperature and therefore the rate of activity; if there is too little water, the microorganisms will die.

When food is exposed to air, moisture and warmth, microorganisms will quickly grow on it. Storing food in dry, cold conditions prevents microorganisms and fungi from growing.

Food Preservation

Microorganisms will feed on any source of food and cause it to decay if the conditions are right.

Food can be preserved by removing the oxygen, heat or moisture that the microorganisms need in order to survive:

- Food can be sealed inside sterile cans or bottles to prevent microorganisms from getting any oxygen (e.g. sealing beans in tins).
- Food can be kept at low temperatures to slow down the growth of microorganisms (e.g. keeping food in a fridge or freezer).
- Food can be pickled in vinegar; its low pH slows down the growth of microorganisms by destroying the microorganisms' enzymes (e.g. pickling onions in vinegar).
- Adding sugar (or salt) to a food makes the conditions too concentrated for the microorganisms to survive (e.g. adding sugar to fruit to make jam).
- Drying food reduces the moisture available to microorganisms preventing them from growing (e.g. drying pasta and beans).

More About Decay

The ideal conditions for the microorganisms that cause decay are those that increase their respiration, growth and reproduction rates.

Temperature – as the temperature is increased, the microorganisms' rate of respiration and growth increases until it reaches 40°C, which is the optimum temperature (i.e. at this temperature the microorganisms' growth and respiration rates are as high as they can be). Above 40°C, the microorganisms are denatured, so decay stops.

Amount of oxygen – increasing the amount of oxygen in the air increases the microorganisms' rate of respiration, which means they produce more energy, enabling them to grow and reproduce more quickly. There is no optimum amount of oxygen: the more there is, the better.

Amount of water – microorganisms grow quickest in moist conditions, which increases the rate of decay. Having too much or too little water present slows down their growth and, therefore, the rate of decay.

Bacteria and fungi are **saprophytes** – they feed on dead organic material by secreting enzymes onto their food and then absorbing the digested products. Saprophytes are essential for decay.

Decay

Food Preservation (cont.)

Example

An experiment can be carried out to show that decay is caused by microorganisms (see diagram alongside). Follow this method:

1. Pour a solution containing nutrients into Flask A.
2. Melt and shape the neck of the flask.
3. Boil the nutrient solution to kill microorganisms and drive out air.
4. Seal the neck of the flask. Pour more of the same nutrient solution into another flask (Flask B), but this time snap off the neck.

The solution that is in the flask that had the neck snapped off (Flask B) will start to decay within days because microorganisms will be able to enter the flask, but the solution in the other flask (Flask A) will show no signs of decay as long as it remains sealed.

Decomposers

When dead organisms or waste materials decay, minerals are released which can then be re-used by other living organisms.

Various soil organisms, including bacteria, fungi, earthworms, maggots and woodlice, help with the process of decay.

Earthworms, woodlice and maggots are known as detritivores; they feed on dead organisms and the waste (detritus) produced by living organisms. Detritivores speed up the process of decay because they break detritus down into small particles which have a large surface area, making it easier for decomposers to feed on. The faeces of detritivores provide food for decomposers like bacteria and fungi.

Decomposer organisms (microorganisms) are used by humans to break down waste:

- they feed on human waste in sewage treatment works
- they break down plant waste in compost heaps.

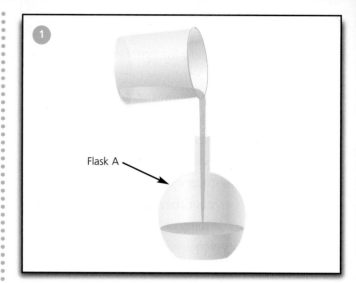

Flask A

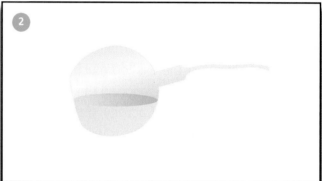

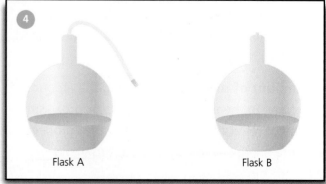

Flask A   Flask B

Recycling

In a stable community, the processes which remove materials are balanced by processes which return materials. So materials are constantly being recycled. For example, when animals and plants grow they take in elements from the soil which are incorporated into their bodies. Then, when they die and decay, these mineral elements are released and can be taken up by other living organisms to enable them to grow. Carbon and nitrogen are two of the elements which are recycled.

The Carbon Cycle

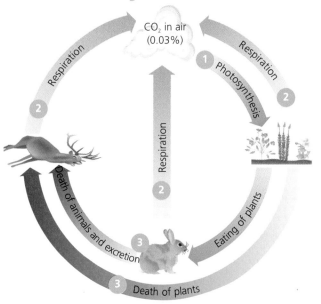

The constant recycling of carbon is called the **carbon cycle** (see diagram opposite).

1. Carbon dioxide is removed from the atmosphere by green plants for photosynthesis.
2. Plants and animals respire releasing carbon dioxide into the atmosphere.
3. Microorganisms feed on dead plants and animals, causing them to break down and decay and release carbon dioxide into the air. (The microorganisms respire as they feed.)

> HT Bacteria and fungi are decomposers. They feed on dead animals and plants and then respire, which releases carbon dioxide into the air.
>
> Carbon is also recycled in the sea (see diagram below):
> 1. Marine organism shells are made of carbonates. The shells drop to the sea bed as the organisms die.
> 2. The shells fossilise to become limestone rock.
> 3. Volcanic eruptions heat the limestone and release carbon dioxide into the atmosphere.
> 4. Acid rain weathers buildings and rocks, releasing carbon dioxide.

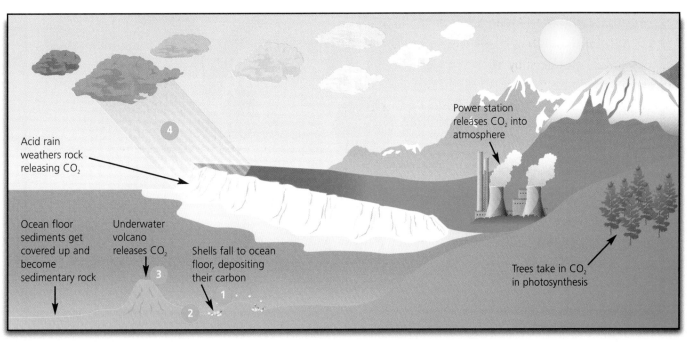

Recycling

The Nitrogen Cycle

The air contains approximately 78% nitrogen. Nitrogen is a vital element of all living things and is used in the production of proteins, which are needed for growth in plants and animals. The nitrogen cycle (see diagram opposite) shows how nitrogen and its compounds are recycled in nature:

1. Plants absorb nitrates from the soil to make protein for growth.
2. Animals eat plants and use the nitrogen to make animal protein.
3. Dead animals and plants are broken down by decomposers, releasing nitrates back into the soil.

There is a lot of nitrogen stored in the air, but animals and plants cannot use it because it is so unreactive.

The Role of Bacteria in the Cycle

Nitrogen-fixing bacteria convert atmospheric nitrogen into nitrates in the soil. Some of these bacteria live free in the soil while some are associated with the root systems of certain plants.

Nitrifying bacteria convert ammonium compounds into nitrates in the soil.

Denitrifying bacteria convert nitrates into atmospheric nitrogen, and ammonium compounds into atmospheric nitrogen.

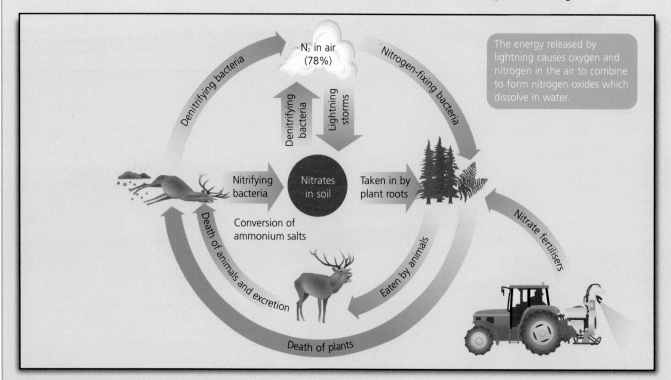

Fundamental Chemical Concepts

By now you should be familiar with all the fundamental chemical concepts, but turn back to p.22–24 to refresh your memory.

In addition, you need to know the formulae for the following compounds:

Acids
- Hydrochloric acid, HCl
- Nitric acid, HNO_3
- Sulfuric acid, H_2SO_4

Carbonates
- Calcium carbonate, $CaCO_3$
- Sodium carbonate, Na_2CO_3

Chlorides
- Ammonium chloride, NH_4Cl
- Barium chloride, $BaCl_2$
- Potassium chloride, KCl
- Silver chloride, AgCl
- Sodium chloride, NaCl

Hydroxides
- Potassium hydroxide, KOH
- Sodium hydroxide, NaOH

Sulfates
- Ammonium sulfate, $(NH_4)_2SO_4$
- Barium sulfate, $BaSO_4$
- Potassium sulfate, K_2SO_4
- Sodium sulfate, Na_2SO_4

Others
- Ammonia, NH_3
- Copper (II) oxide, CuO
- Silver nitrate, $AgNO_3$

Universal Indicator Solution

Acids and Bases

Acids and Bases

Acids are substances that have a pH of less than 7. **Bases** are the oxides and hydroxides of metals. The bases that are soluble are called **alkalis**, and they have a pH greater than 7.

The pH of a solution can be determined by using **universal indicator**. You just need to add a few drops of the solution to the substance and compare the resulting colour to the chart below.

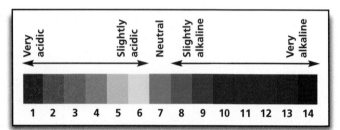

Neutralisation

Acids and bases (alkalis) are chemical opposites. If they are added together in the correct amounts they can cancel each other out. This is called **neutralisation** because the solution that remains has a neutral pH of 7.

Acid **+** Base ⟶ Salt **+** Water

For example, adding hydrochloric acid (HCl) to potassium hydroxide (KOH):

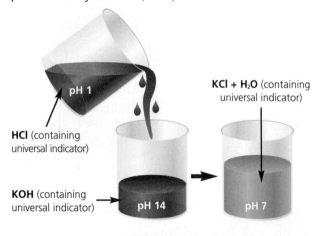

HCl (containing universal indicator)

KOH (containing universal indicator) → pH 14

pH 1

KCl + H₂O (containing universal indicator) → pH 7

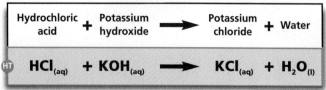

| Hydrochloric acid | + | Potassium hydroxide | ⟶ | Potassium chloride | + | Water |

$$HCl_{(aq)} + KOH_{(aq)} \longrightarrow KCl_{(aq)} + H_2O_{(l)}$$

As the acid is gradually added to the alkali, the **pH** of the solution **decreases**. This is because the acid neutralises the alkali to reach a pH of 7.

The opposite occurs if an alkali is added to an acid, i.e. the **pH** of the solution **increases** as the alkali neutralises the acid to reach a pH of 7.

Carbonates neutralise acids to produce a salt and water, but they also produce carbon dioxide gas.

Acid **+** Carbonate ⟶ Salt **+** Water **+** Carbon dioxide

Naming Salts

The first name of a salt made by neutralisation comes from the first name of the base or carbonate used, for example...

- **sodium** hydroxide will make a **sodium** salt
- **copper** oxide will make a **copper** salt
- **calcium** carbonate will make a **calcium** salt
- **ammonia** will make an **ammonium** salt.

The second name of the salt comes from the acid used, for example...

- hydro**chlor**ic acid will produce a **chlor**ide salt
- **sulf**uric acid will produce a **sulf**ate salt
- **nitr**ic acid will produce a **nitr**ate salt.

For example, adding **potassium** hydroxide to **nitr**ic acid to neutralise it will make **potassium nitrate**.

Sulfuric Acid

Millions of tonnes of sulfuric acid are used every year in the UK, for example...

- to clean metals before they are painted or coated
- to neutralise fertilisers
- in car and motorbike batteries.

More on Neutralisation

Neutralisation can be summarised by looking at what happens to the ions in the solutions:

- alkalis in solution contain **hydroxide ions**, $OH^-_{(aq)}$
- acids in solution contain **hydrogen ions**, $H^+_{(aq)}$.

Neutralisation can therefore be described using the ionic equation...

$$H^+_{(aq)} + OH^-_{(aq)} \longrightarrow H_2O_{(l)}$$

You should be able to construct any of the following word equations and balanced formula equations for producing salts:

Acid + Base $\longrightarrow$ Salt + Water

	Hydrochloric Acid $(HCl_{(aq)})$	Sulfuric Acid $(H_2SO_{4(aq)})$	Nitric Acid $(HNO_{3(aq)})$
Sodium Hydroxide $(NaOH_{(aq)})$	Sodium chloride + Water	Sodium sulfate + Water	Sodium nitrate + Water
	$NaOH_{(aq)} + HCl_{(aq)}$ $\longrightarrow NaCl_{(aq)} + H_2O_{(l)}$	$2NaOH_{(aq)} + H_2SO_{4(aq)}$ $\longrightarrow Na_2SO_{4(aq)} + 2H_2O_{(l)}$	$NaOH_{(aq)} + HNO_{3(aq)}$ $\longrightarrow NaNO_{3(aq)} + H_2O_{(l)}$
Potassium Hydroxide $(KOH_{(aq)})$	Potassium chloride + Water	Potassium sulfate + Water	Potassium nitrate + Water
	$KOH_{(aq)} + HCl_{(aq)}$ $\longrightarrow KCl_{(aq)} + H_2O_{(l)}$	$2KOH_{(aq)} + H_2SO_{4(aq)}$ $\longrightarrow K_2SO_{4(aq)} + 2H_2O_{(l)}$	$KOH_{(aq)} + HNO_{3(aq)}$ $\longrightarrow KNO_{3(aq)} + H_2O_{(l)}$
Copper (II) Oxide $(CuO_{(s)})$	Copper (II) chloride + Water	Copper (II) sulfate + Water	Copper (II) nitrate + Water
	$CuO_{(s)} + 2HCl_{(aq)}$ $\longrightarrow CuCl_{2(aq)} + H_2O_{(l)}$	$CuO_{(s)} + H_2SO_{4(aq)}$ $\longrightarrow CuSO_{4(aq)} + H_2O_{(l)}$	$CuO_{(s)} + 2HNO_{3(aq)}$ $\longrightarrow Cu(NO_3)_{2(aq)} + H_2O_{(l)}$

Acid + Base $\longrightarrow$ Salt

	Hydrochloric Acid $(HCl_{(aq)})$	Sulfuric Acid $(H_2SO_{4(aq)})$	Nitric Acid $(HNO_{3(aq)})$
Ammonia $(NH_{3(aq)})$	Ammonium chloride	Ammonium sulfate	Ammonium nitrate
	$NH_{3(aq)} + HCl_{(aq)}$ $\longrightarrow NH_4Cl_{(aq)}$	$2NH_{3(aq)} + H_2SO_{4(aq)}$ $\longrightarrow (NH_4)_2SO_{4(aq)}$	$NH_{3(aq)} + HNO_{3(aq)}$ $\longrightarrow NH_4NO_{3(aq)}$

Acid + Carbonate $\longrightarrow$ Salt + Water + Carbon Dioxide

	Hydrochloric Acid $(HCl_{(aq)})$	Sulfuric Acid $(H_2SO_{4(aq)})$	Nitric Acid $(HNO_{3(aq)})$
Sodium Carbonate $(Na_2CO_{3(s)})$	Sodium chloride + Water + Carbon dioxide	Sodium sulfate + Water + Carbon dioxide	Sodium nitrate + Water + Carbon dioxide
	$Na_2CO_{3(s)} + 2HCl_{(aq)}$ $\longrightarrow 2NaCl_{(aq)} + H_2O_{(l)} + CO_{2(g)}$	$Na_2CO_{3(s)} + H_2SO_{4(aq)}$ $\longrightarrow Na_2SO_{4(aq)} + H_2O_{(l)} + CO_{2(g)}$	$Na_2CO_{3(s)} + 2HNO_{3(aq)}$ $\longrightarrow 2NaNO_{3(aq)} + H_2O_{(l)} + CO_{2(g)}$
Calcium Carbonate $(CaCO_{3(s)})$	Calcium chloride + Water + Carbon dioxide	Calcium sulfate + Water + Carbon dioxide	Calcium nitrate + Water + Carbon dioxide
	$CaCO_{3(s)} + 2HCl_{(aq)}$ $\longrightarrow CaCl_{2(aq)} + H_2O_{(l)} + CO_{2(g)}$	$CaCO_{3(s)} + H_2SO_{4(aq)}$ $\longrightarrow CaSO_{4(aq)} + H_2O_{(l)} + CO_{2(g)}$	$CaCO_{3(s)} + 2HNO_{3(aq)}$ $\longrightarrow Ca(NO_3)_{2(aq)} + H_2O_{(l)} + CO_{2(g)}$

Reacting Masses

Relative Atomic Mass, A_r

Atoms are too small for their actual atomic mass to be of much use to us. A more useful measure is **relative atomic mass, A_r**. This is the mass of a particular atom compared to the mass of an atom of hydrogen (the lightest atom).

N.B. A twelfth of the mass of a carbon atom is now used instead of the mass of hydrogen, but it does not make a difference.

Each element in the periodic table has two numbers. The larger of the two numbers (top left) is the A_r of the element.

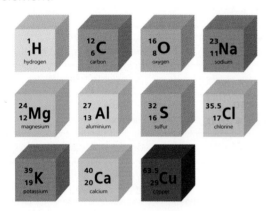

Relative Formula Mass, M_r

The **relative formula mass**, M_r, of a compound is simply the A_rs of all its elements added together. To calculate the M_r we need the formula of the compound and the A_r of all the atoms involved.

There are a number of ways to set out an M_r calculation. Whichever method you choose, you should always show your working. The simplest method is shown below:

Example 1
Calculate the relative formula mass of H_2SO_4.

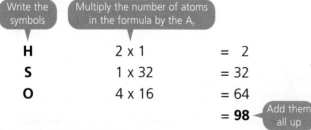

H	2 x 1	= 2
S	1 x 32	= 32
O	4 x 16	= 64
		= **98**

Add them all up

The M_r of H_2SO_4 is 98.

Example 2
Calculate the relative formula mass of $Ca(OH)_2$.

Ca	1 x 40	= 40
O	2 x 16	= 32
H	2 x 1	= 2
		74

The M_r of $Ca(OH)_2$ is 74.

Calculating the Amount of Reactants and Products

To calculate how much product a reaction will produce or how much reactant you need, you need to remember these important ideas:
- the total mass of the starting materials (reactants) always equals the total mass of the substances produced (products)
- the more reactant you start with the greater the amount of product you will make
- substances react in simple ratios.

You can use the ratio to calculate how much of each reactant you will need in order to produce a certain amount of product.

Example
Nitric acid and ammonia react with each other to make ammonium nitrate:

Nitric acid ➕ **Ammonia**	➡	**Ammonium nitrate**

They react in the ratio 63 : 17. In other words…

a) Calculate how much of each reactant you would need to make 80kg of product.

Use the ratio

63kg	17kg	80kg
Nitric acid	Ammonia	Ammonia nitrate

b) Calculate how much of each reactant you would need to make 16g of product.

$16g = \frac{80g}{5}$, so divide all the quantities by 5

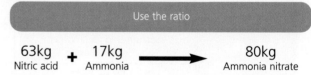

HT More Calculations

The total mass of reactants equals the total mass of products because when a chemical reaction occurs **no atoms are gained or lost**. You end up with exactly the same number as you started with; they are just rearranged into different substances.

We sometimes need to be able to work out how much of a substance is used up or produced in a chemical reaction. To do this we need to know…
- the relative formula mass, M_r, of the reactants and products (or the relative atomic mass, A_r, of all the elements)
- the balanced symbol equation for the reaction.

By substituting the M_rs into the balanced equation, we can work out the ratio of mass of reactant to mass of product and apply this to the question.

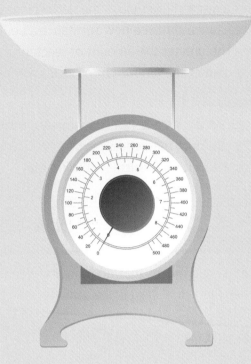

Example 1
When calcium carbonate ($CaCO_3$) is heated, it produces calcium oxide (CaO) and carbon dioxide (CO_2). How much calcium oxide can be produced from 50kg of calcium carbonate?

(Relative atomic masses: Ca = 40, C = 12, O = 16.)

> Write down the equation.

$$CaCO_{3(s)} \xrightarrow{heat} CaO_{(s)} + CO_{2(g)}$$

> Work out the M_r of each substance.

$$40 + 12 + (3 \times 16) \longrightarrow (40 + 16) + [12 + (2 \times 16)]$$

> Check that the total mass of reactants equals the total mass of the products. If they are not the same, check your work.

$$100 \longrightarrow 56 + 44 ✔$$

> Since the question only mentions calcium oxide and calcium carbonate, you can now ignore the carbon dioxide. This gives the ratio of mass of reactant to mass of product.

$$100 : 56$$

> Apply this ratio to the question…

If 100kg of $CaCO_3$ produces 56kg of CaO, then 1kg of $CaCO_3$ produces $\frac{56}{100}$ kg of CaO and 50kg of $CaCO_3$ produces $\frac{56}{100} \times 50$ = **28kg** of CaO.

Example 2
Aluminium (Al) and oxygen (O_2) are produced from aluminium oxide (Al_2O_3). How much aluminium oxide is needed to produce 540 tonnes of aluminium?

(Relative atomic masses: Al = 27, O = 16.)

> Write down the equation.

$$2Al_2O_{3(l)} \longrightarrow 4Al_{(l)} + 3O_{2(g)}$$

> Work out the M_r of each substance.

$$2 [(2 \times 27) + (3 \times 16)] \longrightarrow (4 \times 27) + [3 \times (2 \times 16)]$$

> Check that the total mass of reactants equals the total mass of the products.

$$204 \longrightarrow 108 + 96 ✔$$

> Since the question only mentions aluminium oxide and aluminium carbonate, you can now ignore the oxygen.

$$204 : 108$$

> Apply this ratio to the question…

If 204 tonnes of Al_2O_3 produces 108 tonnes of Al, then $\frac{204}{108}$ tonnes is needed to produce 1 tonne of Al and $\frac{204}{108} \times 540$ tonnes is needed to produce 540 tonnes of Al, i.e. **1020 tonnes** of Al_2O_3 is needed.

Reacting Masses

Percentage Yield

Whenever a reaction takes place, the starting materials, i.e. the reactants, produce new substances, i.e. the products. The greater the amount of reactants used, the greater the amount of products formed.

Percentage yield is a way of comparing the actual amount of product made (the actual yield) to the amount of product theoretically expected, which is the predicted yield. It is calculated using the following formula:

$$\text{Percentage yield} = \frac{\text{Actual yield}}{\text{Predicted yield}} \times 100$$

- A 100% yield means that no product has been lost, i.e. the actual yield is the same as the predicted yield.
- A 0% yield means that no product has been made, i.e. the actual yield is zero.

Example 1

A reaction was carried out and the actual yield was 8g. The predicted yield was 10g. Calculate the percentage yield.

Use the formula…

$$\text{Percentage yield} = \frac{\text{Actual yield}}{\text{Predicted yield}} \times 100$$

$$= \frac{8g}{10g} \times 100 = \mathbf{80\%}$$

Example 2

A reaction was carried out to produce the salt magnesium sulfate. The predicted yield of magnesium sulfate was 7g while the actual yield was 4.9g.

Calculate the percentage yield of magnesium sulfate.

$$\text{Percentage yield} = \frac{\text{Actual yield}}{\text{Predicted yield}} \times 100$$

$$= \frac{4.9g}{7g} \times 100 = \mathbf{70\%}$$

In Example 2, the percentage yield of magnesium sulfate was 70% which means that some magnesium sulfate was lost during the reaction. It could have been lost during evaporation, filtration, the transfer of liquids and/or heating.

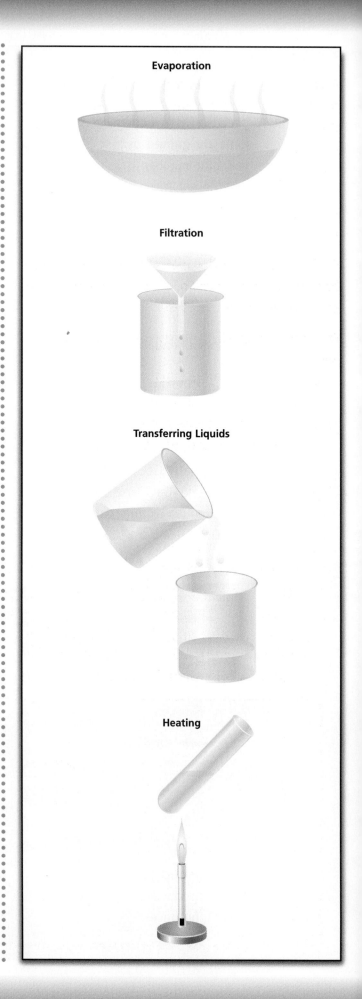

Evaporation

Filtration

Transferring Liquids

Heating

Fertilisers

Fertilisers are chemicals that farmers use in order to provide their plants with the **essential elements** they need for growth. They make crops grow faster and bigger and they increase the crop yield. The three main essential elements found in fertilisers are…

- nitrogen, N
- phosphorus, P
- potassium, K.

Fertilisers must be soluble in water so that they can be taken in by the roots of plants in solution. **Urea** can also be used as a fertiliser.

Fertilisers that can be made by neutralising an acid with an alkali are…

- ammonium sulfate, which is manufactured by neutralising sulfuric acid with ammonia
- ammonium nitrate, which is manufactured by neutralising nitric acid with ammonia

- ammonium phosphate, which is manufactured by neutralising phosphoric acid with ammonia
- potassium nitrate, which is manufactured by neutralising nitric acid with potassium hydroxide.

You need to be able to calculate the relative formula mass of a fertiliser if you are given its chemical formula.

Example

Calculate the M_r of the fertiliser that is represented by the chemical formula NH_4NO_3.

Calculate the M_r of NH_4NO_3 in the usual way.

N	2 x 14	= 28
H	4 x 1	= 4
O	3 x 16	= 48
		M_r = **80**

ᴴᵀ Making a Fertiliser

To make a fertiliser (e.g. potassium nitrate), follow these steps (see diagrams below):

1 Measure out the alkali (e.g. potassium hydroxide) into a basin using a measuring cylinder.

2 Add acid (e.g. nitric acid) from a burette. Use a glass rod to put a drop of solution onto indicator paper to test the pH. Continue to add the acid a bit at a time until the solution is neutral (pH 7).

3 Evaporate the solution slowly until crystals form on the end of a cold glass rod placed in the solution. Leave to cool and crystallise.

4 Filter to separate the crystals from the solution.

5 Remove the crystals, wash them and leave to dry.

This method is another example of producing a salt (a fertiliser) from neutralisation (see p.72).

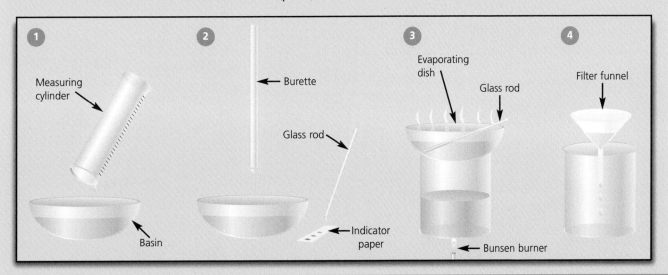

Fertilisers and Crop Yield

More About Fertilisers

Fertilisers increase crop yield by replacing essential elements in the soil that have been used up by a previous crop, or by increasing the amount of essential elements available. More importantly, they provide nitrogen in the form of **soluble nitrates** which are used by the plant to make protein for growth.

Eutrophication

Careless overuse of fertilisers can cause stretches of nearby water to become stagnant very quickly. This process is called **eutrophication**.

1 Fertilisers used by farmers may be washed into lakes and rivers, which increases the level of nitrates and phosphates in the water and increases the growth of simple algae.

Algae

2 The algal bloom blocks off sunlight to other plants, causing them to die and rot.

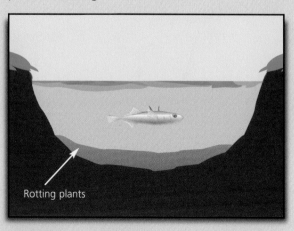
Rotting plants

3 This leads to a massive increase in the number of aerobic bacteria (which feed on dead organisms), which quickly use up the oxygen. Eventually, nearly all the oxygen is removed. This means there is not enough left to support the larger organisms, such as fish and other aquatic animals, causing them to suffocate.

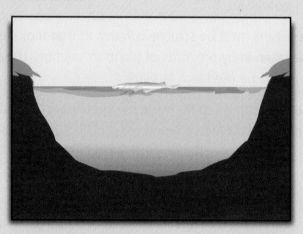

Percentage Mass

To calculate the percentage mass of an element in a compound like a fertiliser, use the following formula...

$$\text{Percentage mass} = \frac{\text{Mass of element}}{\text{Relative formula mass}} \times 100$$

Example

What is the percentage mass of nitrogen in ammonium nitrate (NH_4NO_3) fertiliser?

First calculate the M_r of NH_4NO_3.

N	2 x 14	= 28
H	4 x 1	= 4
O	3 x 16	= 48
		M_r = **80**

So the mass of 2 atoms of nitrogen is 28 and the M_r is 80. You can now calculate the percentage mass of nitrogen in the compound...

$$\frac{A_r \text{ N}}{M_r \text{ NH}_4\text{NO}_3} \times 100$$

$$= \frac{28}{80} \times 100 = \textbf{35\%}$$

Ammonia

Ammonia (NH_3) is an alkaline gas. It is made from nitrogen and hydrogen. Getting these gases to chemically combine and stay combined is very difficult. This is because the reaction is reversible: as well as nitrogen and hydrogen combining to form ammonia, the ammonia decomposes in the same conditions to form hydrogen and nitrogen.

Reversible reactions have the symbol ⇌ in their equation to show that the reaction can take place in either direction.

Ammonia can be used to make cleaning fluids, nitric acid and fertilisers. Farmers rely on cheap fertilisers made from ammonia to produce enough food for an ever-growing world population.

The Haber Process

Fritz Haber was the first to work out how to make ammonia on a large scale. The raw materials are nitrogen (obtained from the air) and hydrogen (from natural gas or the cracking of crude oil).

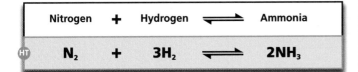

The mixture of 1 part nitrogen and 3 parts hydrogen is compressed to a high pressure of 200 atmospheres and passed into a reactor. The gases are passed over an iron catalyst at 450°C. This is where the reaction takes place (see diagram below).

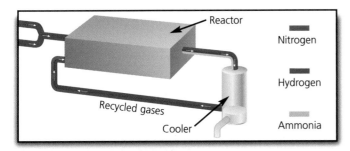

About 28% of the gases are converted into ammonia, which is separated from the unreacted hydrogen and nitrogen by cooling, and collected as a liquid. The unreacted gases are recycled.

Optimum conditions are not used in the Haber process as they would be too expensive to maintain, so a compromise is reached.

Example

Interpret the graph and table below to explain how temperature and pressure affect the rate of reaction in the Haber process.

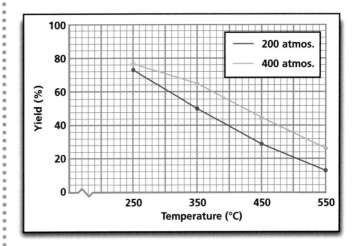

% Yield	Temperature			
Pressure	250°C	350°C	450°C	550°C
200 atmos.	73%	50%	28%	13%
400 atmos.	77%	65%	45%	26%

From the above information you should be able to pick out, for example, that the yield falls when temperature is increased and that the yield increases as pressure increases.

> (HT) You may also be asked to interpret data on other industrial processes in terms of rate, percentage yield and cost.

Cost

The cost of making a new substance depends on…
- the price of energy (gas and electricity)
- labour costs (wages for employees)
- how quickly the new substance can be made
- cost of starting materials (reactants)
- cost of equipment needed (plant and machinery).

Making Ammonia – Haber Process

Factors Affecting Cost

There are various factors that affect the cost of making a new substance, including…
- the pressure required – the higher the pressure the higher the plant cost
- the temperature required – the higher the temperature the higher the energy cost

- the catalysts required – catalysts reduce costs because they increase the rate of reaction, but they need to be purchased in the first place which increases initial costs.
- the number of people required to operate machinery – automation reduces the wages bill
- the amount of unreacted material that can be recycled – recycling reduces costs.

Economic Considerations

Economic considerations determine the conditions used in the manufacture of chemicals:
- the **rate of reaction** must be high enough to produce a sufficient daily yield of product
- **percentage yield** achieved must be high enough to produce a sufficient daily yield of product (a low percentage yield is acceptable providing the reaction can be repeated many times with **recycled starting materials**)
- **optimum conditions** should be used to give the most economical reaction (this could mean producing a slower reaction or a lower percentage yield at a lower cost).

Economics of the Haber Process

There is great economic importance attached to producing the maximum amount of ammonia in the shortest possible time at a reasonable cost. This demands a degree of compromise.

Effect of Temperature

$$N_2 + 3H_2 \underset{\text{Endothermic}}{\overset{\text{Exothermic}}{\rightleftharpoons}} 2NH_3$$

The formation of ammonia is exothermic so a low temperature would favour the production of ammonia, i.e. the forward reaction, which would increase the yield. Increasing the temperature increases the rate of reaction in both directions (the ammonia forms faster and breaks down faster), but reduces the yield.

Effect of Pressure

Increased pressure means increased concentration and, therefore, a faster reaction rate.

Also, since four molecules are being changed into two molecules, increasing the pressure favours the smaller volume. Therefore, high pressure favours the production of ammonia. However, too high a pressure is expensive to maintain and contain.

Effect of a Catalyst

Using a catalyst increases the rate of the reaction, although it does not affect the percentage yield. However, although using a catalyst can reduce costs, purchasing it increases initial costs.

A Summary
- A low temperature increases yield but the reaction is too slow.
- A high pressure increases yield but the reaction is too expensive.
- A catalyst increases the rate of reaction but does not change the percentage yield.

A Compromise

A compromise is reached in the Haber process…
- temperature – 450°C
- pressure – 200 atmospheres
- catalyst – iron.

You may be asked to use the above ideas to interpret how rate, cost and yield affect other industrial processes.

Washing Powder

A washing powder is a **mixture**. The main components are…

- detergent – to do the cleaning
- bleach – to remove coloured stains
- water softener – to soften hard water (hard water contains soluble calcium and magnesium compounds that react with soap)
- optical brightener – to make whites appear brighter
- enzymes – to break up food and protein stains in low-temperature washes.

When clothes are washed, the water is the **solvent** (the liquid that does the dissolving), and the washing powder is the **solute** (the solid that gets dissolved) because it is soluble (i.e. it dissolves) in water. The resulting mixture of solvent and solute is a **solution**.

Low-temperature washes are used to wash delicate fabrics, i.e. ones that would shrink in a hotter wash or that have a dye that could run, and they do not denature enzymes in biological powders. An advantage of low-temperature washes is that they save energy.

You can find out which washing conditions your clothes require by looking at the symbols on the labels:

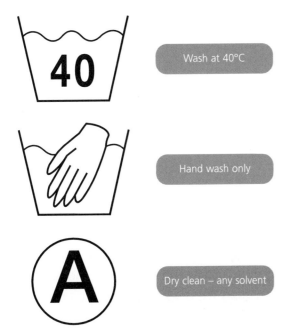

Some stains will not dissolve in water; they are **insoluble**. Dry cleaning solvents are used when a stain is insoluble in water. The clothes are still washed in a liquid but it does not contain water. Different solvents will dissolve different stains (see table below).

Stain	Solvent
Ball-point pen	Methylated spirits (ethanol) then biological washing powder in water
Blood	Biological washing powder in water
Shoe polish	White spirit then biological washing powder in water
Coffee	Biological washing powder in water
Correcting fluid	White spirit

You do not have to remember the details of this table but you may be asked to use similar information to choose which solvent to use to remove a stain.

Washing-Up Liquid

Washing-up liquid contains…

- detergent – to do the cleaning
- water – to dissolve and dilute the detergent so that it pours out of the bottle
- water softener – to soften hard water
- rinse agent – to help the water drain off the crockery so it dries quickly
- colour and fragrance – to make the product more attractive to buy.

The detergent in a washing-up liquid is often a salt made by neutralising a complicated organic acid with an alkali.

Acid **+** Alkali ⟶ Salt (detergent) **+** Water

In your exam you may be asked to interpret data about the effectiveness of washing-up liquids and washing powders. The data could be presented in a table or a graph.

Detergents

Detergent Molecule

A detergent molecule (see diagram below) is **non-polar**, i.e. the molecule has a balanced overall charge.

However, when the molecule is dissolved in water, the sodium ion comes away from the 'head' of the molecule.

The sodium ion is positively charged, which leaves the 'head' of the detergent molecule negatively charged.

The charged 'head' is attracted to water molecules because of its polarity (electrical charge), so it is known as **hydrophilic** (water-loving).

The hydrocarbon tail is non-polar and so it is not attracted to water molecules. It is therefore known as **hydrophobic** (water-hating).

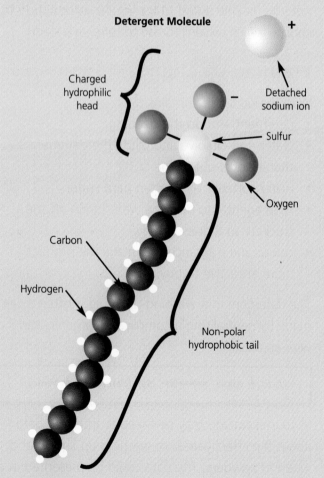

Detergent Molecule

Charged hydrophilic head

Detached sodium ion

Sulfur

Oxygen

Carbon

Hydrogen

Non-polar hydrophobic tail

How Detergents Work

The diagram below shows how the detergents in washing-up liquid work.

1 The hydrophobic end of the detergent molecule is repelled by the water, causing it to stick to the oil droplet.

2 As more and more detergent molecules are absorbed into the oil droplet, the oil is eventually lifted off the plate.

3 When it is totally surrounded, the oil droplet can be washed away, leaving the plate clean.

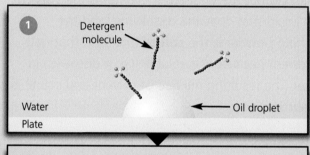

Detergent molecule

Water

Plate

Oil droplet

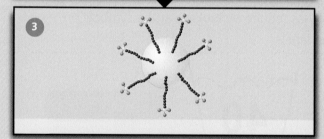

Dry-Cleaning Solvents

The molecules that make up a stain are held together by weak **intermolecular forces** (attractive forces between the molecules). The stain substance will dissolve in a dry-cleaning solvent if the intermolecular forces that hold it together are overcome. The new intermolecular forces between the stain molecules and the solvent molecules are stronger than the ones that were present before.

Batch and Continuous

In a batch process, the reactants are put into a reactor, the reaction happens and then the product is removed. Medicines and pharmaceutical drugs are often made in batches. Batch processes…
- make a product on demand
- make a product on a small scale
- can be used to make a variety of products
- are more labour intensive because the reactor needs to be filled, emptied and cleaned.

In a continuous process, e.g. the Haber process, reactants are continually being fed into a large reactor and the product is continually being produced at the same time (like a conveyer belt). Continuous processes…
- operate all the time
- make a product on a large scale
- are dedicated to just one product
- can run automatically.

Making Medicines

The materials used to make a medicine can be **manufactured** (synthetic) or they can be extracted from **natural sources** such as plants. The steps needed to extract a small amount of material from a plant source are as follows:

1. **Crushing** – the plant material is crushed using a mortar and pestle.

2. **Dissolving** – a suitable solvent is added to dissolve the material.

3. **Chromatography** – a concentrated solution of the material is spotted onto chromatography paper and allowed to separate.

Developing Medicines

It takes a long time – over 10 years – from discovering a material that will act as a medicine, to being able to use it on patients.

Research needs to be carried out into new pharmaceutical materials. This cannot be automated (carried out by machines) as decisions need to be made, so highly qualified staff are needed. This means that labour costs are high.

Further research is then carried out to **develop** the drug to increase its effectiveness before it is **tested** to ensure it works properly, is safe to use and has no serious side-effects. The medicine must then be approved for use and must satisfy all the **legal requirements** set out by the government before it can be sold.

Medicines are expensive because the materials could be rare or may require complex methods to extract the **raw materials** (starting materials) from plants. Medicines are made in small quantities and it is not possible to totally automate the manufacturing process and, therefore, energy and staff costs are high. The marketing of a new medicine is also very expensive.

More on Developing Medicines

The research and development of a new pharmaceutical material may take a few years but it takes longer to carry out the safety tests, including testing on human volunteers. There are very strict legal rules which a new medicine must satisfy before it can be put on the market. A pharmaceutical company may invest hundreds of millions of pounds to develop one medicine and the company will have a limited time to recoup this investment before their exclusive right to produce the medicine runs out. If the number of people using the medicine is small then the cost would be very high.

Nanochemistry

Carbon

There are three forms of carbon…
* diamond (see below)
* graphite (see below)
* buckminster fullerene (buckyball) (see p.85).

Diamond

Diamond has a rigid structure (see diagram below). It…
* does not conduct electricity
* is insoluble in water
* is used in jewellery because it is colourless, clear (transparent) and lustrous (shiny)
* can be used in cutting tools because it is very hard and has a very high melting point.

Graphite

Graphite has a layered structure (see diagram below right). It…
* is insoluble in water
* is black, which is why it is used in pencils
* is lustrous and opaque (light cannot travel through it)
* conducts electricity and has a very high melting point, so is used to make electrodes for electrolysis
* is slippery, so it is used in lubricants.

More on Carbon

Diamond, graphite and the fullerenes (see p.85) are **allotropes** of carbon. Allotropes are different forms of the same element where the atoms are arranged in different molecular structures.

More on Diamond

Diamond is a giant molecule made of carbon atoms that are bonded to four other carbon atoms by strong covalent bonds. The large number of covalent bonds results in diamond having a high melting point. It does not have any free electrons so it does not conduct electricity. Unlike graphite, it does not have separate layers and, because there are strong covalent bonds between the carbon atoms, it is very hard.

More on Graphite

Graphite is a giant molecule which exists in layers of carbon atoms that are bonded to three other carbon atoms by strong covalent bonds. The layers are held together by weak intermolecular forces, allowing each layer to slide easily, so graphite can be used as a lubricant. The presence of free (delocalised) electrons in graphite results in it being an electrical conductor. It has a high melting point because it has many strong covalent bonds to break.

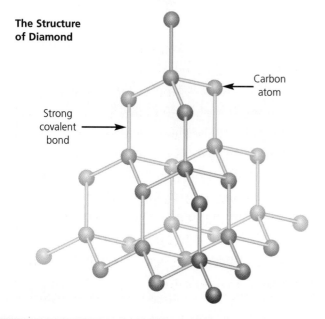

The Structure of Diamond

Carbon atom

Strong covalent bond

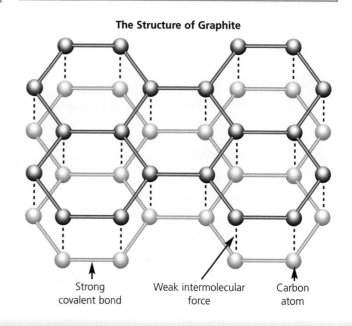

The Structure of Graphite

Strong covalent bond

Weak intermolecular force

Carbon atom

Nanochemistry

Nanochemistry deals with materials on an atomic scale (i.e. individual atoms), whereas chemistry is usually concerned with much larger quantities. The properties of particles on this very small scale are very different to the properties of the bulk material. Researchers in nanochemistry are very interested in the element **carbon** because of the properties it has at the atomic scale. Two forms of carbon that nanochemists are interested in are the buckminster fullerene and nanotubes.

Buckminster Fullerene

A buckminster fullerene (C_{60}) consists of 60 carbon atoms arranged in a sphere. It is named after the architect Richard Buckminster Fuller, who popularised domes. It…

- is a black solid
- makes a red solution when dissolved in petrol.

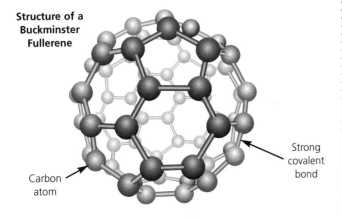

Structure of a Buckminster Fullerene

Carbon atom

Strong covalent bond

Nanotubes

The discovery of the buckminster fullerene led chemists to investigate building similar structures.

In the early 1990s the first **nanotubes** were made by joining fullerenes together. They look like sheets of graphite hexagons curled over into a tube.

Nanotubes conduct electricity and are very strong. They are used to…

- reinforce graphite tennis rackets because of their strength
- make connectors and semiconductors in the most modern molecular computers because of their electrical properties
- develop new, more efficient industrial catalysts.

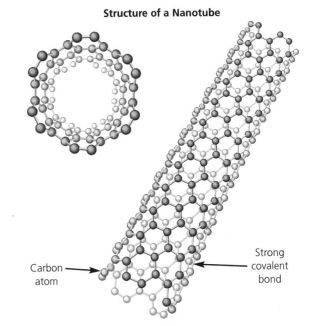

Structure of a Nanotube

Carbon atom

Strong covalent bond

HT More on Nanochemistry

Fullerenes and nanotubes can be used to cage other molecules because they are the perfect shape to trap other substances inside them. The caged substances can be…

- **drugs**, e.g. a major new HIV treatment uses buckyballs to deliver a material which disrupts the way in which the HIV virus works
- **catalysts** – by attaching catalyst material to a nanotube, a massive surface area can be achieved, making the catalyst very efficient.

Fullerenes and nanotube molecules are manufactured by a variety of processes:

- Buckyballs were first discovered in the soot produced by burning hydrocarbons. This method of manufacture is still common. The hydrocarbon fuel is burned under low pressure and the hydrogen burns off leaving behind the carbon.
- Lasers can be used to vaporise carbon which then deposits onto a molecule and builds up the structure piece by piece.
- Matter can be removed from a big structure to produce nanoscale features.

Water

The four main **sources** of water are...

- rivers
- lakes
- reservoirs
- aquifiers (wells and bore holes).

Example

The pie chart shows the sources of water in Northern Ireland.

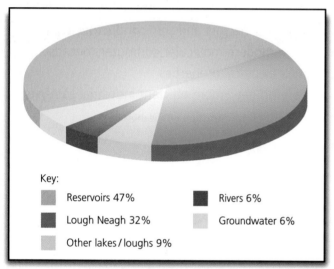

Key:

■ Reservoirs 47%		■ Rivers 6%	
■ Lough Neagh 32%		■ Groundwater 6%	
■ Other lakes / loughs 9%			

You will not be expected to remember this data, but you may be asked to interpret data like this. For example, using this data you could be asked to pick out the largest water source in Northern Ireland.

Water is an important resource for industry as well as being essential for drinking, washing and other jobs in the home. The chemical industry uses large amounts of water for **cooling**, as a **solvent** and as a **raw material**.

In some parts of Britain the demand for water is higher than the supply, so it is important not to waste water.

We take clean water (i.e. water without disease-carrying microorganisms) for granted, but many parts of the developing world still do not have clean water. The World Health Organisation estimates that over 2 million people worldwide die every year from water-borne diseases and that nearly 20% of the world's population does not have access to clean drinking water.

Water Treatment

Water has to be **treated** to **purify** it and make sure it is safe to drink before it reaches the home or factory. Untreated (raw) water can contain...

- insoluble particles
- pollution
- microorganisms
- dissolved salts and minerals.

A typical treatment process is shown below:

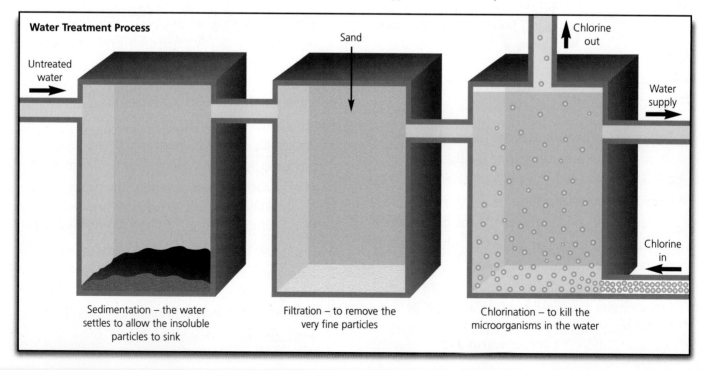

Water Treatment Process

Untreated water

Sand

Chlorine out

Water supply

Chlorine in

Sedimentation – the water settles to allow the insoluble particles to sink

Filtration – to remove the very fine particles

Chlorination – to kill the microorganisms in the water

Pollution in Water

The **pollutants** that may be found in water supplies include nitrates from the run-off of fertilisers; lead compounds from old pipes in the plumbing; and pesticides from spraying crops near to the water supply. These materials are more difficult to remove from the water.

The table below shows some pollutants and the maximum amounts permitted in drinking water.

Pollutant	Maximum Amount Permitted
Nitrates	50 parts in 1 000 000 000 parts water
Lead	50 parts in 1 000 000 000 parts water
Pesticides	0.5 parts in 1 000 000 000 parts water

Again, you do not have to remember the data but you may be asked to pick out which pollutant has the smallest allowed concentration, or transfer this data onto a graph.

Dissolved Ions

The **dissolved ions** of some salts are easy to identify as they will undergo **precipitation** reactions. A precipitation reaction occurs when a solid is made from mixing two solutions together.

Sulfates can be detected using barium chloride solution: a white precipitate of barium sulfate forms. For example…

Sodium sulfate	+	Barium chloride	→	Barium sulfate (white)	+	Sodium chloride

$$^{HT} Na_2SO_{4(aq)} + BaCl_{2(aq)} \rightarrow BaSO_{4(s)} + 2NaCl_{(aq)}$$

Silver nitrate solution is used to detect halide ions. Halides are the ions made by the halogens (Group 7).

With silver nitrate…
- chlorides form a white precipitate
- bromides form a cream precipitate
- iodides form a pale yellow precipitate.

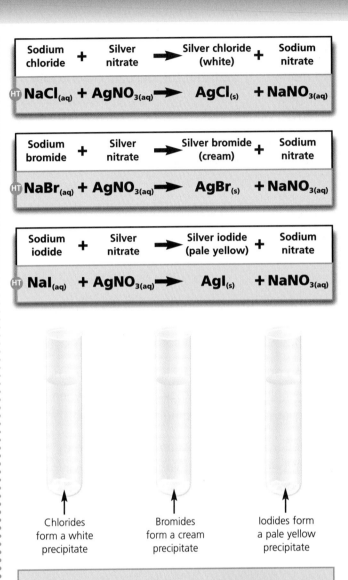

Sodium chloride	+	Silver nitrate	→	Silver chloride (white)	+	Sodium nitrate

$$^{HT} NaCl_{(aq)} + AgNO_{3(aq)} \rightarrow AgCl_{(s)} + NaNO_{3(aq)}$$

Sodium bromide	+	Silver nitrate	→	Silver bromide (cream)	+	Sodium nitrate

$$^{HT} NaBr_{(aq)} + AgNO_{3(aq)} \rightarrow AgBr_{(s)} + NaNO_{3(aq)}$$

Sodium iodide	+	Silver nitrate	→	Silver iodide (pale yellow)	+	Sodium nitrate

$$^{HT} NaI_{(aq)} + AgNO_{3(aq)} \rightarrow AgI_{(s)} + NaNO_{3(aq)}$$

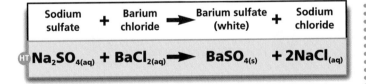

Chlorides form a white precipitate

Bromides form a cream precipitate

Iodides form a pale yellow precipitate

More on Water Purification

Tap water is not pure. It contains soluble materials that are not removed by the normal water treatment process. There is the possibility that some of the materials may be poisonous and, in that case, extra steps must be taken to remove them. Water must be distilled to make sure it is absolutely pure. This uses lots of energy, so it is very costly.

Huge amounts of expensive energy would be needed in order to distil sea water. And because sea water is quite corrosive, the equipment needed would be very costly. These factors make the cost for making drinking water out of sea water prohibitive, i.e. we are prevented from doing it because the cost is too high.

Sparks

Generating Static Electricity

An **insulating material** can become **electrically charged** if it is rubbed with another insulating material. The charge is **static electricity**; the electricity stays on the material and does not move. This is due to the **transfer of electrons** from one material to the other, leaving one material with a **positive** charge and the other with a **negative** charge.

You can generate static electricity by rubbing a balloon against a jumper. The electrically charged balloon will then attract very small objects, e.g. pieces of paper or cork. The same effect can be obtained using a rubbed comb or strip of plastic.

Dusting brushes can use this effect. The brushes can be charged so that they attract dust when they pass over it, making dusting more effective.

Synthetic clothing can become charged up by friction between the clothing and the person's body when the clothes are put on. When the clothing is later removed from the body, static sparks are sometimes produced.

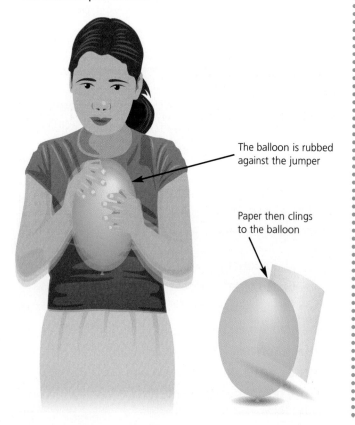

The balloon is rubbed against the jumper

Paper then clings to the balloon

Discharging Static Electricity

A charged object can be **discharged** (i.e. have any charge on it removed) by **earthing** it.

When an object discharges, electrons are transferred from the charged object to earth.

If you become charged, earthing can result in you getting an **electrostatic shock**.

Getting Out of a Car
A person can become charged up in a car due to friction between the seat and their body. When they get out of the car and touch it after it has been driven, discharge can occur, resulting in an electrostatic shock.

Touching Water Pipes
A person can become charged up by friction between the soles of their feet and the floor if they are walking on an insulator such as carpet or vinyl. If they then touch a water pipe, e.g. a radiator, the charge is earthed. Discharge occurs, resulting in an electrostatic shock.

Problems of Static Electricity

Some places, such as flour mills and petrochemical factories, have atmospheres that contain extremely flammable gases or high concentrations of oxygen. A discharge of static electricity (i.e. a spark) in these situations can lead to an **explosion**, so factories take precautions to ensure that no spark is made that could ignite the gases.

Static electricity is also dangerous in any situation where large quantities could flow through your body to earth: lightning, for example.

In other situations, static electricity is not dangerous but can be a nuisance, for example...

- it can cause dirt and dust to be attracted to insulators such as television screens and computer monitors
- it can cause some materials to cling to your skin.

Repulsion and Attraction

Two insulating materials with the **same charge** will **repel** each other, e.g. two Perspex rods.

For example, if a positively charged rod is held near to a suspended rod which is positively charged, the suspended rod is repelled. The same effect would happen if both rods had a negative charge.

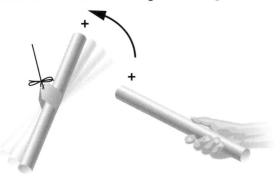

Two insulating materials with **different charges** will **attract** each other, e.g. a Perspex and an ebonite rod.

If a negatively charged rod is held near to a suspended rod which is positively charged, the suspended rod is attracted to it. The same effect would happen if the charges were the other way round.

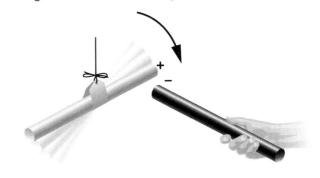

Why Objects Become Charged Up

Electric charge (static) builds up when **electrons** (which have a **negative charge**) are rubbed off one material onto another. The material that **receives** the electrons becomes **negatively** charged due to an excess of electrons, while the material **giving up** the electrons becomes **positively** charged due to a loss of electrons.

Example 1

If you rub a Perspex rod with a cloth, the Perspex gives up electrons and becomes positively charged. The cloth receives the electrons and becomes negatively charged.

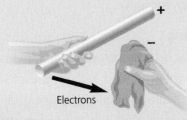

Electrons

Example 2

If you rub an ebonite rod with fur, the fur gives up the electrons and becomes positively charged. The ebonite receives electrons and becomes negatively charged.

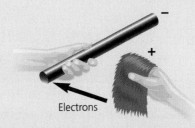

Electrons

Reducing the Danger

The chance of receiving an electric shock can be reduced by…

• ensuring appliances are correctly earthed
• using insulation mats effectively
• wearing shoes with insulating soles.

Lorries that contain inflammable gases, liquids or powders need to be earthed before unloading, as friction can cause a build-up of charge. This charge could lead to a spark, which could then ignite the flammable substance.

Anti-static sprays, liquids and cloths help to reduce the problems of static electricity by preventing the transfer of charge from one insulator to another. With no build-up of charge, there can be no discharge.

Uses of Electrostatics

Using Static in Everyday Life

Static electricity is used in many ways in everyday life. The following are some examples:

Photocopiers

An image of the page to be copied is projected onto an electrically charged plate, which usually has a positive charge.

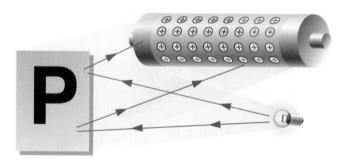

Light causes charge to leak away, leaving an electrostatic impression of the page.

The charged impression on the plate attracts tiny specks of black powder, which are then transferred from the plate to paper. Heat is used to fix the final image on the paper.

Laser Printers

A printer cartridge contains a rotating drum which is charged up. As the drum rotates, a laser beam discharges parts of the drum to leave behind an image of text and graphics. The drum then rotates past charged toner which is attracted to the discharged parts of the drum. The toner is then transferred from the drum onto paper, which is heated to fix the final image.

Defibrillators

Static electricity can be used to start the heart when it has stopped. Two paddles are charged and are put in good electrical contact with the patient's chest. Charge is then passed through the patient to make the heart contract. However, care must be taken not to shock the operator.

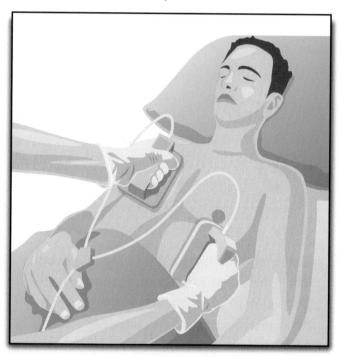

Reducing Smoke Particles in Chimneys

Static electricity is used in electrostatic dust precipitators to remove smoke particles from chimneys. Metal plates / grids are installed in the chimney and are connected to a high voltage (potential difference). The dust particles are attracted to the plate / grid, where they form larger particles that fall back down the chimney when they are heavy enough.

Spray Painting

The panel that is to be sprayed is made positively charged. It is then sprayed with negatively charged paint from a negatively charged paint gun. The paint particles repel each other, but are attracted to the positively charged panel. This causes the paint to form a fine spray so it is applied evenly. It also means that less paint is wasted and even the back and sides of the object that would be in the shadow of the spray receive a coat of paint.

Circuits

A **circuit** is a complete loop that allows an electrical current to flow. Electrons flow around the circuit from the negative electrode of the power source to the positive electrode. However, this was only discovered recently so circuit diagrams show the current flowing from the positive to the negative electrode.

Fuses and Circuit Breakers

Fuses and circuit breakers (devices that act like a fuse, but can be reset) are both **safety devices** that can be used to prevent fires, injury and death in the home by **breaking the circuit** of an appliance if a fault occurs.

How a Fuse Works

A fuse is a short, thin piece of wire with a low melting point. It is used to prevent cables or appliances from overheating. This is how it works:

1. A fault causes the current in the appliance to exceed the current rating of the fuse.
2. The fuse wire gets hot and melts or breaks.
3. The circuit is broken so no current can flow.
4. The appliance is protected.

However, for this safety system to work properly, the **current rating** of the fuse must be **just above** the normal current that flows through the appliance.

Example of a Fuse in Action

If the current flowing through an appliance is below the current rating of the fuse, the appliance will work properly (see diagram 1). However, if a fault occurs inside the appliance and the live wire makes contact with the neutral wire (see diagram 2), the current flowing would then be higher than the current rating of the fuse because there would be less resistance. This causes the fuse wire to get hotter and hotter until it melts and breaks the circuit (see diagram 3), which prevents current from flowing so there is no danger of the flex overheating (which would result in a fire). Further damage to the appliance or injury to the user is prevented.

Summary

Fuses and circuit breakers...
- prevent fires as they do not allow cables and flexes to overheat
- prevent injury and death as they do not allow appliances to become 'live'
- prevent damage to the components of an appliance as they do not allow a current to flow which is greater than the normal current that flows through the appliance.

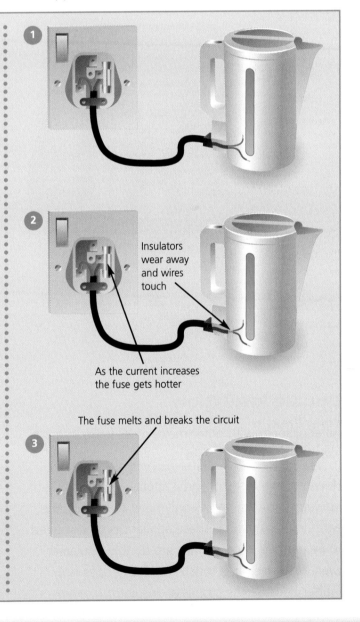

Insulators wear away and wires touch

As the current increases the fuse gets hotter

The fuse melts and breaks the circuit

Safe Electricals

Live, Neutral and Earth Wires

Most electrical appliances are connected to the mains electricity supply using a cable and 3-pin plug which is inserted into a socket on the ring main circuit.

Most cables contain three wires:

- **live wire (brown)** – carries current to the appliance at a high voltage: about 230V (fuses, circuit breakers and switches are always part of the live wire circuit)
- **neutral wire (blue)** – completes the circuit and carries current away from the appliance
- **earth wire (green and yellow)** – safety wire that stops the appliance becoming live.

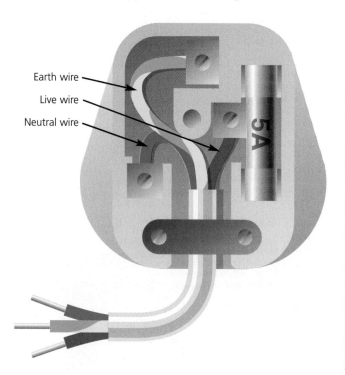

Earth wire
Live wire
Neutral wire
5A

Double Insulation

All appliances with outer metal cases have an earth wire, i.e. they are earthed.

However, the cases of some appliances are made of insulators so their cables only need two wires; the earth wire is missing. These appliances do not need to be earthed because they are double insulated; even if the live parts touch the case it does not matter because the case is an insulator.

Earthing

All electrical appliances with outer metal cases must be earthed to protect the appliance and the user. The outer case of the appliance is connected to the earth pin in the plug through the earth wire. This is how it works:

1. A fault in the appliance causes the casing to become live.
2. The circuit short-circuits (i.e. the path of the flow of charge changes) because the earth wire offers less resistance.
3. The fuse wire melts (or the circuit breaker trips).
4. The circuit is broken.
5. The appliance and the user are protected.

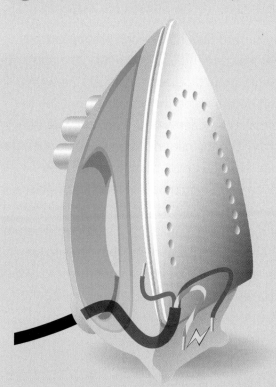

Double-insulated appliances do not need earthing. Unlike the iron above, the cases of these appliances are insulators and cannot become live. Also, all metal parts inside the appliance are insulated from the outer case.

They may not have an earth wire but they are still protected by a fuse.

Fixed and Variable Resistors

Resistance is a measure of how hard it is to get a **current** through a component in a circuit at a particular voltage (potential difference). It is measured in ohms (Ω).

The current through a circuit can be controlled by varying the resistance in the circuit. This can be done by using…

- a **fixed resistor** – a component whose resistance is constant. The bigger its resistance, the smaller the current that flows for a particular voltage

Fixed resistor – high resistance   Fixed resistor – low resistance

- a **variable resistor** (also known as a rheostat) – a component whose resistance can be altered. The current that flows can be changed by simply moving the sliding contact of the variable resistor from one end to the other, as shown below.

Variable resistor – high resistance   Variable resistor – low resistance

Current, Voltage and Resistance

Current, voltage and resistance are related by the following formula:

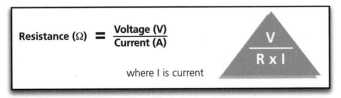

Resistance (Ω) $=$ $\dfrac{\text{Voltage (V)}}{\text{Current (A)}}$

$$\frac{V}{R \times I}$$

where I is current

- For a given resistor, current increases as voltage increases (and vice versa).
- For a fixed voltage, current decreases as resistance increases (and vice versa).

Example 1

Calculate the resistance of the lamp in the following circuit:

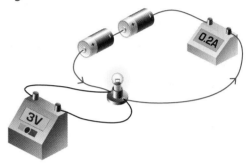

Use the formula…

$$\text{Resistance} = \frac{\text{Voltage}}{\text{Current}}$$
$$= \frac{3V}{0.2A}$$
$$= \mathbf{15\Omega}$$

HT As well as being able to recall the formula opposite, you should be able to rearrange it to calculate potential difference or current.

Example 2

Calculate the reading on the ammeter in the circuit below if the bulb has a resistance of 20 ohms.

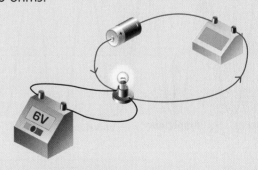

Rearrange the formula…

$$\text{Current} = \frac{\text{Voltage}}{\text{Resistance}}$$
$$= \frac{6V}{20\Omega}$$
$$= \mathbf{0.3A}$$

Ultrasound

Ultrasound

Ultrasound is the name given to sound waves that have frequencies greater than 20 000 hertz (Hz), i.e. above the upper threshold of the human hearing range.

Ultrasound travels in a **longitudinal** wave. Longitudinal waves can be demonstrated using a slinky spring (see diagram below).

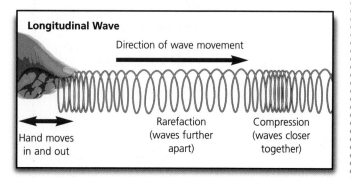

The key features of waves (as shown in the diagram below) are…

- **amplitude** – the maximum disturbance caused by a wave
- **wavelength** – the distance between corresponding points on two successive disturbances
- **frequency** – the number of waves produced (or that pass a particular point) in 1 second.

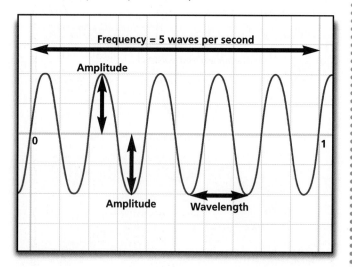

Applications of Ultrasound

Ultrasound can be used in medicine to look inside people, e.g. to scan bodies, measure the speed of blood flow, and break down stones (e.g. kidney stones).

Breaking Down Kidney Stones

Ultrasound waves can be used to break down kidney stones in the body so they can be removed without the need for painful surgery (see diagram below).

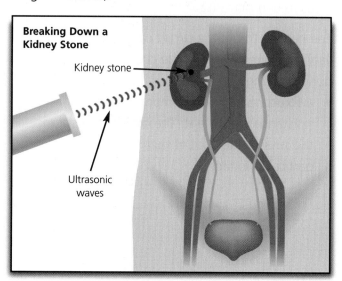

> **HT** Ultrasonic waves cause the kidney stones to vibrate making them break up and disperse. They are then passed out of the body in urine.

Body Scans

Ultrasound waves are used to build up a picture of the organs in the body, including the heart, lungs and liver. They can also be used to detect gallstones and tumours. They are used for pre-natal scanning (see diagram below) because there is no risk to either the mother or the baby.

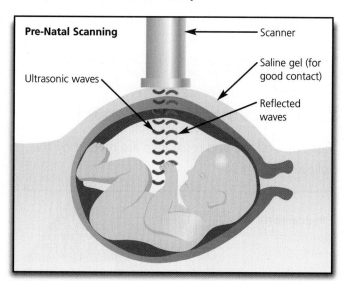

More on Ultrasound

Ultrasound waves are partly reflected at a boundary as they pass from one medium or substance into another. The time taken for these reflections to be detected can be used to calculate the depth of the reflecting surface. The reflected waves are usually processed to produce a visual image on a screen.

Ultrasound has two main advantages over X-ray imaging:

- it is able to produce images of soft tissue
- it does not damage living cells.

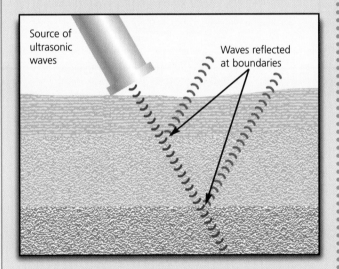

Motion of Particles in Waves

All waves **transfer energy** from one point to another **without transferring any particles** of matter. If we allow each coil of the slinky spring opposite to represent one particle, then we can show the movement of the particles in each wave.

Longitudinal Waves

Each particle moves backwards and forwards about its normal position in the same plane as the direction of wave movement.

Transverse Waves

Each particle moves up and down about its normal position at right angles (90°) to the direction of the wave movement.

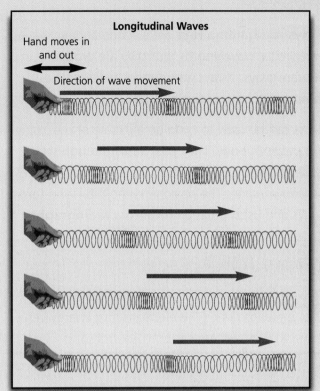

Longitudinal Waves

Hand moves in and out

Direction of wave movement

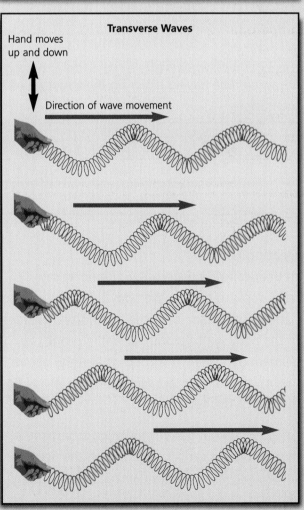

Transverse Waves

Hand moves up and down

Direction of wave movement

Treatment

Radiation

X-rays and **gamma rays** are electromagnetic waves with similar wavelengths, but they are produced in different ways. X-rays and nuclear radiation (i.e. **gamma** and **beta radiation**) can be used in medicine.

X-rays can be used to build up a picture of the inside of a patient's body. They pass easily through soft tissue and less easily through bone, which produces a shadow image. The person in a hospital who takes X-rays and uses radiation is called a **radiographer**.

Gamma and beta radiation can pass through skin and damage cells. These can be useful properties:

- gamma rays damage cells, so they can be used to treat cancer
- beta and gamma rays pass through skin, so they can be used as medical tracers (to track the tracer's progress through a patient's system).

Gamma rays can also be used to **sterilise** medical equipment because they kill germs and bacteria.

More About Radiation

X-rays are made by firing high-speed electrons at metal targets. (The electrons lose energy very quickly.) X-rays are easier to control than gamma rays.

After alpha or beta decay, a nucleus sometimes contains surplus energy. It emits this as gamma radiation, which is very high frequency electromagnetic radiation. Unlike alpha or beta decay, gamma has no effect on the structure of the nucleus.

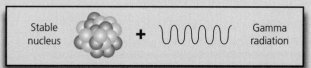

Stable nucleus + Gamma radiation

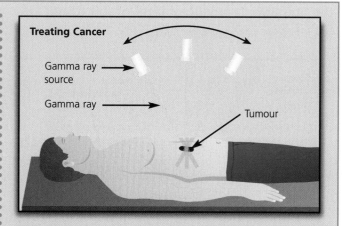

Treating Cancer
Gamma ray source
Gamma ray
Tumour

Uses of Gamma Rays

Treating Cancer

To treat cancer a wide beam of gamma rays from a source outside the body is focused on the tumour. The beam is rotated around the outside of the body with the tumour at the centre (see diagram opposite). This concentrates the gamma rays on the tumour, but minimises the effects on the rest of the body.

An advantage of gamma radiation treatment is that it destroys cancer cells without the need for surgery. However, it may damage other (healthy) cells and cause sickness.

Tracers

A tracer is a small amount of a radioactive material which is put into a patient so that its progress through the body can be followed using a radiation detector outside the body.

The radioactive material must emit either gamma or beta radiation as both of these are capable of passing out of the body to be detected.

The tracer can be swallowed or injected into the body. After it is administered, it is then given time to spread through the patient's body.

For example, the thyroid gland in the neck is an important organ as it influences the metabolic rate of the body. Iodine is absorbed in the thyroid gland, so a patient is given a radioactive substance which contains iodine-131. A detector can then be used to follow its progress. We can find out how well the thyroid gland is working by measuring the amount of iodine it absorbs.

Radioactivity

Radioactive materials give out **nuclear radiation** from the **nucleus** of their atoms because they are **unstable** and therefore decay (break down).

During decay, radiation can be given out in the form of **alpha**, **beta** and **gamma rays**:

- an alpha particle is a helium nucleus, i.e. two protons and two neutrons
- a beta particle is a fast-moving electron
- a gamma ray is an electromagnetic wave.

Radiation is measured by the number of nuclear decays emitted per second. This number decreases with time.

Alpha Emission

During **alpha emission**, the atom decays by **ejecting** an alpha particle (a **helium** nucleus made up of two protons and two neutrons) from the nucleus. A new atom is formed by alpha decay.

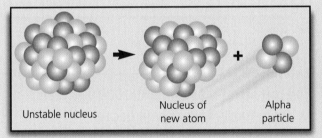

| Unstable nucleus | Nucleus of new atom | Alpha particle |

The nucleus of the new atom differs from the original one in the following ways:

- it is a different element
- it has 2 fewer protons and 2 fewer neutrons
- the atomic number has decreased by 2
- the mass number has decreased by 4.

For example, the alpha decay of radium-226 into radon-222 is shown by the following equation:

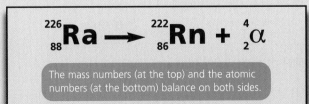

$$^{226}_{88}\text{Ra} \longrightarrow \, ^{222}_{86}\text{Rn} + \, ^{4}_{2}\alpha$$

The mass numbers (at the top) and the atomic numbers (at the bottom) balance on both sides.

Beta Emission

During **beta emission**, the atom decays by **changing a neutron** into a **proton** and an **electron**. The high-energy electron which is ejected from the nucleus is a beta particle. A new atom is formed by beta decay.

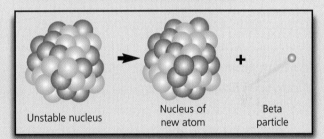

| Unstable nucleus | Nucleus of new atom | Beta particle |

The nucleus of the new atom differs from the original one in the following ways:

- it is a different element
- it has 1 more proton and 1 less neutron
- the atomic number has increased by 1
- the mass number remains the same.

For example, the beta decay of iodine-131 into xenon-131 is shown by the following equation:

$$^{131}_{53}\text{I} \longrightarrow \, ^{131}_{54}\text{Xe} + \, ^{0}_{-1}\beta$$

Again, the mass numbers and the atomic numbers balance on both sides.

What is Radioactivity?

HT Half-Life

Half-life is the time it takes for half the undecayed nuclei in a radioactive substance to decay. If the substance has a very long half-life then it remains active for a very long time.

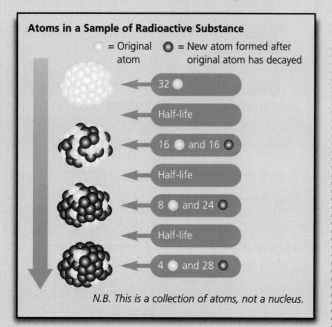

Igneous rocks can contain uranium atoms which decay via a series of relatively short-lived (unstable) atoms to produce stable atoms of lead. This takes a long time because uranium has a very long half-life. By measuring the proportion of uranium and lead in the rock and knowing the half-life of uranium, it is possible to date the rock.

Calculations Involving Half-Life

The half-life of a substance can be calculated using a table or a graph.

Example 1

The table below shows the activity (measured in becquerels, Bq) of a radioactive substance against time.

Time (min)	0	5	10	15	20	25	30
Activity (Bq)	200	160	124	100	80	62	50

a) Calculate the half-life of the substance by using a table.

To find an average, choose three pairs of points between which the activity has halved.

Activity	Time	Half-Life
200 → 100	0 → 15	15 min
160 → 80	5 → 20	15 min
100 → 50	15 → 30	15 min

The half-life is **15 minutes**.

b) Calculate the half-life by drawing a graph.

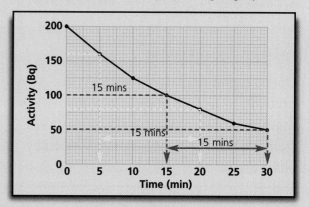

The half-life is **15 minutes**.

Example 2

The half-life of uranium is 700 000 000 years. Uranium forms lead when it decays.

A sample is found to contain three times as much lead as uranium. Calculate the age of the sample.

The fraction of lead present is $\frac{3}{4}$, while the fraction of uranium present is $\frac{1}{4}$. (There is three times as much lead as uranium.)

$$
\begin{array}{ccccc}
\text{Fraction of} & & \text{Fraction of} & & \text{Original amount} \\
\text{lead} & + & \text{uranium} & = & \text{of uranium} \\
\frac{3}{4} & + & \frac{1}{4} & = & 1
\end{array}
$$

Work out the number of decays it takes to get $\frac{1}{4}$:

$$1 \xrightarrow{\text{half-life}} \frac{1}{2} \xrightarrow{\text{half-life}} \frac{1}{4} \quad \longleftarrow \text{2 half-lives}$$

Age of rock = 2 x half-life

= 2 x 700 000 000 years

= **1 400 000 000 years**

Background Radiation

Background radiation occurs **naturally** in our environment and is around us all the time. Most is released by radioactive substances in **soil** and **rocks**. **Cosmic rays** from outer space also contribute significantly to background radiation.

Tracers

Radioisotopes are used as tracers in industry as well as in hospitals. They are used to find out what is happening inside objects without having to break the objects open. In industry, tracers are used to…
• track the dispersal of waste
• find leaks and blockages in underground pipes
• find the routes of underground pipes.

Smoke Alarms

Most smoke alarms contain americium-241 which is an alpha emitter. Emitted particles cause the air particles to ionise and the ions formed are attracted to the oppositely charged electrodes. This results in a current flowing in the circuit.

When smoke enters the space between the two electrodes, less ionisation takes place as the alpha particles are absorbed by the smoke particles. This causes a smaller current than normal to flow, and the alarm sounds.

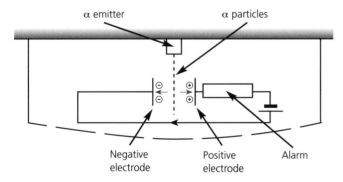

Carbon Dating

A small amount of the carbon in our atmosphere and in the bodies of animals and plants is radioactive carbon-14. Measurements from radioactive carbon can be used to date old materials and rocks.

More on Background Radiation

Not all background radiation occurs naturally. A small proportion comes from **waste products** and **man-made** sources. Industry and hospitals are both responsible for contributing to today's background radiation levels.

More on Tracers

A radioactive material that emits gamma rays is put into the pipe. A gamma source is used because gamma can penetrate through to the surface. The progress of the material is tracked by a detector above ground:
• if there is a **leak**, the radioactive material will **escape** and will be detected at the surface
• if there is a blockage, the radioactive material will **stop flowing** so it cannot be detected after this point.

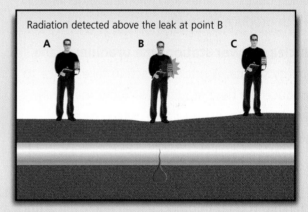
Radiation detected above the leak at point B

More on Carbon Dating

The amount of radioactive carbon-14 in the atmosphere has not changed for thousands of years. When an object dies it no longer exchanges gases with the air as living matter does. Therefore, as the carbon-14 in the dead object decays, the radioactivity of the sample decreases. This means that the dead object has a different radioactivity to living matter. The ratio of these two activities can be used to find a fairly accurate approximate age for the object.

Fission

Producing Electricity

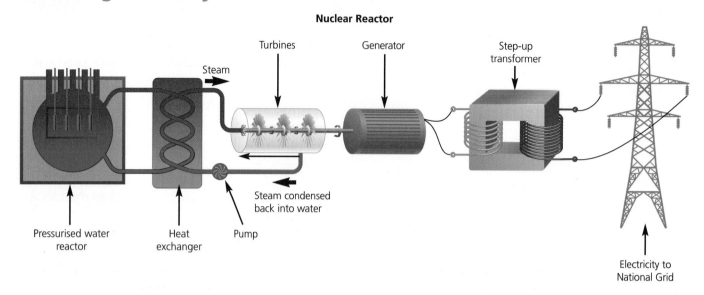

Nuclear Reactor

Turbines · Generator · Step-up transformer

Steam

Steam condensed back into water

Pressurised water reactor · Heat exchanger · Pump

Electricity to National Grid

Conventional power stations use **fossil fuels**, i.e. coal, oil and gas, as an energy source to generate electricity. The fuel is burned to release heat energy to boil water. This produces steam which drives turbines and, ultimately, generators which produce electricity.

Nuclear power stations use **uranium** as the energy source. A nuclear reaction takes place to produce the heat required to create the steam, which again turns a turbine, which turns a generator, to produce electricity.

Fission

Uranium is used to produce heat energy in a nuclear reactor. This process is called **nuclear fission**. The decay of uranium can be a **chain reaction**.

Absorbing a single neutron is enough to cause the uranium nucleus to split, releasing heat energy and more neutrons. These neutrons cause more uranium nuclei to split and so the chain reaction continues (see p.101).

A **nuclear bomb** is a chain reaction that has gone **out of control**, resulting in the release of one powerful burst of energy.

Nuclear fission produces radioactive waste, which can be very dangerous.

Nuclear Fission

Nuclear fission is the process used in nuclear reactors to produce energy to make electricity.

On a Small Scale
Bombarding a uranium atom with a neutron causes the nucleus to split and energy is released as a result (see diagram on p.101).

On a Large Scale
When a neutron collides with a very large nucleus (e.g. uranium), the nucleus splits up into two smaller nuclei (e.g. barium and krypton). This releases more than one neutron, capable of causing further fission.

This is a chain reaction, so it carries on and on and on (see diagram on p.101).

Scientists stop nuclear reactions getting out of control by placing **control rods** in the reactor.

The control rods **absorb** some of the **neutrons** (preventing further fissions).

The control rods can be lowered or raised to control the number of neutrons available for fission, which allows the process to keep operating safely.

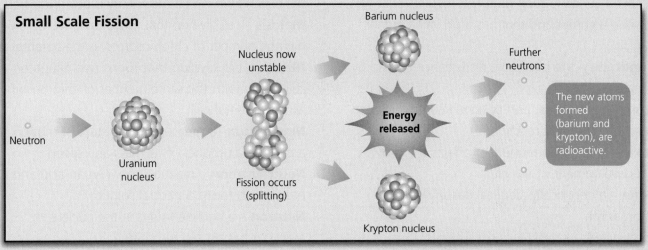 Nuclear Fission (cont.)

Small Scale Fission

Neutron → Uranium nucleus → Nucleus now unstable / Fission occurs (splitting) → Barium nucleus / **Energy released** / Krypton nucleus → Further neutrons

The new atoms formed (barium and krypton), are radioactive.

Large Scale Fission

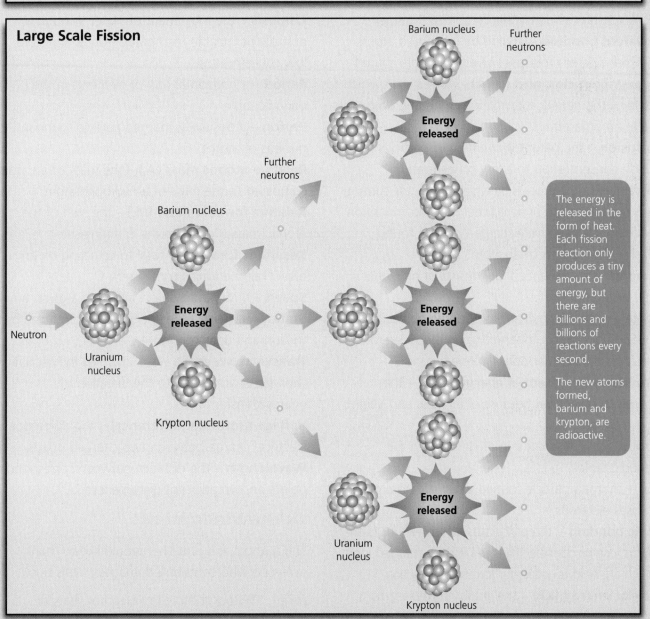

The energy is released in the form of heat. Each fission reaction only produces a tiny amount of energy, but there are billions and billions of reactions every second.

The new atoms formed, barium and krypton, are radioactive.

Glossary

Acid – a compound that has a pH value lower than 7

Active transport – the movement of substances against a concentration gradient; requires energy

Alkali – a compound that has a pH value higher than 7

Amplitude – the maximum disturbance caused by a wave

Atom – the smallest part of an element which can enter into chemical reactions

Auxin – a plant hormone that affects the growth and development of the plant

Clone – a genetically identical descendent of an organism

Compound – a substance consisting of two or more substances chemically combined together

Covalent bonding – a bond between two atoms in which one or more pairs of electrons are shared

Deoxyribonucleic acid (DNA) – nucleic acid which contains the genetic information carried by every cell in an organism

Diffusion – the natural movement of particles from a high concentration to a low concentration

Electrolysis –the process by which an electric current causes a solution to undergo chemical decomposition

Electron – a negatively charged particle found outside the nucleus of an atom

Element – a substance that consists of only one type of atom

Force – a push or pull acting upon an object

Frequency – the number of waves produced (or that pass a particular point) in one second

Gravitational potential energy (GPE) – the energy an object has because of its mass and height above the earth

Group – a vertical column of elements in the periodic table

Ion – charged particle formed when an atom gains or loses electrons

Ionic bonding – the process by which two or more atoms lose or gain electrons to become charged ions which are held together by forces of attraction

Kinetic energy (KE) – the energy possessed by a body due to its movement

Longitudinal wave – an energy-carrying wave in which the movement of the particles is in line with the direction in which the energy is being transferred

Meiosis – cell division that forms daughter cells with half the number of chromosomes as the parental cell

Mitosis – cell division that forms two daughter cells, each with the same number of chromosomes as the parental cell

Momentum –a measure of the state of motion of a body as a product of its mass and speed

Neutralisation – reaction between an acid and a base which forms a neutral solution

Neutron – a particle found in the nucleus of atoms; it has no electric charge

Osmosis – the movement of water through a partially permeable membrane from a high to a low concentration

Period – a horizontal row of elements in the periodic table

Proton – a positively charged particle found in the nucleus of atoms

Relative atomic mass (A_r) – the mass of an atom compared to the mass of a hydrogen atom

Relative formula mass (M_r) – the sum of the atomic masses of all atoms in a molecule

Resultant force – the total force acting on an object (all the forces combined)

Speed – how far an object travels in a given time

Static electricity – electricity that is produced by friction and does not move

Transverse wave – a wave in which the oscillations (vibrations) are at 90° to the direction of energy transfer

Voltage (potential difference) – the difference in electrical charge between two charged points

Wavelength – the distance between corresponding points on two adjacent disturbances

Acknowledgments

The authors and publisher would like to thank everyone who contributed images to this book:

p.72   ©iStockphoto.com / Heather Watson

Artwork supplied by HL Studios

Index

Index